Shells

Sustained by Grace within the Tempest

Steve Heronemus
11/19/2014

ABOUT THE AUTHOR

Steve Heronemus is a husband and father of four who has been living with ALS since 2003. He has been an avid amateur musician, sailor and leader in church and community roles and has received honors as Valparaiso University Distinguished Alumnae for Community Service, Capgemini Community Leader, and Les Turner ALS Foundation Patient of the Year.

Steve invites you into continued conversation at www.steveheronemus.com or www.facebook.com/shellsbook.

ACKNOWLEDGMENTS

Artwork thanks to:
Rob Tucker and Sue Ellen Dubbert

Certain photographs courtesy of:
Trademan Photography

Copyright © 2014 Steve Heronemus

All rights reserved

DEDICATION

For Suzanne, my wife, my immortal beloved, my best friend, and my life's inspiration: You are the wind for my sails, the beacon in my night, and the harbor for my every storm.

For our children Michelle, John, Matthew, and Claire: You are pearls of inestimable value; I am forever grateful you were given to me to care for and treasure. I love you with everything I have, and I am forever proud of the individuals you are.

For the pastors, staff, and disciples of Bethlehem Lutheran Church in St. Charles, Illinois, and the community of Batavia, Illinois: Thank you for your nurture, care support, acceptance, and opportunities to serve.

For my caregiver Alyssa: You are a blessing to me and my family. Your compassion and dedication enable us to live more fully and freely. You are a joy to us and our "adopted" daughter and sister.

Shells : Sustained by Grace within the Tempest

Introduction

Experts say you should write what you know. I happen to be a Christian, so parts of this book are written from that perspective. If you happen to have a different belief system, please know that I have no intent to either offend or exclude you, and I hope you will connect with the message from your own perspective. I believe God sings with one voice, but we all hear the music differently.

Soon after receiving my initial diagnosis, I made a public promise in front of the church council where I served. I vowed that as long as there was strength in my legs I would walk the Lord's Path, that while my hands still worked I would use them for the Lord, and while I still had a voice I would give praise to God for all the gifts He has given me. I am unbelievably grateful that, through these writings (begun by using dictation into voice-recognition software on my computer and completed by using technology that tracks my eye movements to click out one letter at a time on an on-screen keyboard), I can still fulfill the last part of that pledge.

About ALS

I happen to be living with amyotrophic lateral sclerosis (ALS), commonly known as Lou

Gehrig's disease. And since I am living with ALS, everyone around me, most intensely my wife and children, is living with it too.

Recent medical thought describes ALS as a category of progressive neuromuscular diseases, not one single disease. The unknown number of diseases in this category share a common set of symptoms: death of the upper and lower motor neurons which paralyzes all voluntary muscles. This includes muscles controlling hands and arms, legs and feet, swallowing, speech, blinking, eye movement, and breathing. ALS is always fatal, with people normally surviving only three to five years. People with ALS (pALS) normally die from one of three things – starvation due to not being able to chew and swallow sufficient calories; suffocation from muscles no longer initiating breath; or drowning as pneumonia fills the lungs with fluid.

There is no test to determine if one has ALS; in fact, a diagnosis arrived at by careful observation and elimination of all other possibilities can only be confirmed by autopsy. There are known genetic causes for approximately five percent of cases, while the remaining 95% have an unknown number of unknown causes. It can strike people from their teens to their 90s, slightly more males than females, and people of all nations and races. About two of every 100,000 people are stricken, although a significantly higher percentage of Gulf, Afghanistan, and Iraqi war veterans have developed ALS.

I currently need help to stand up, bathe, dress, and walk. I have a feeding tube through which I get all my nutrition, a device to help me breathe, another device to talk, and a power wheelchair. People with ALS are sometimes said to be in a shell, defined by functioning minds locked up inside bodies that refuse to work. Thank you for walking with me on the journey that defies any notion that our lives' circumstances can define who we are.

About the Les Turner ALS Foundation

Thank you for purchasing this book. A portion of your purchase price for Shells will be donated to the Les Turner ALS Foundation. Founded in 1977 by Les Turner, a Chicago-area man with ALS, and his family and friends, the Foundation pioneered multidisciplinary patient and family care and support in combination with support of two world-class research laboratories. Partnering with the Northwestern Feinberg School of Medicine and the James V. Insolia Foundation, the Les Turner / Lois Insolia ALS Center at Northwestern provides services in neurology, pulmonology, occupational therapy, speech therapy, respiratory therapy, dietetics, and clinical trial participation.

The Patient Services arm of the Foundation provides in-home nursing and social worker services as well as support groups for more than 600 patients and their family members. Patient Services also provides ALS education and advocacy, equipment banks for all-too-expensive accessibility tools that are all-too-infrequently covered by insurance, and transportation services between patient homes and the clinic.

Researchers from the two Foundation-sponsored research laboratories have led and published major breakthroughs in the genetic causes of several inherited forms of ALS and in the cellular processes and genetic predispositions involved in ALS progression; they've also developed a mouse model used for drug trials all over the world. The newer second laboratory focuses on understanding what happens to upper motor neurons, which is no small feat as these are located deep in the brain.

For more information on the Les Turner ALS Foundation, please visit lesturnerals.org.

SHELLS

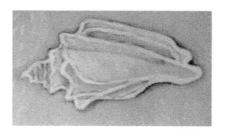

We all have them. Shells are those ways we face the world and our way of living out life within the world. Some shells are gifts given to us by God while others are forced on us by life. Like many things, shells given to us by life are neither good nor bad in and of themselves. It is, rather, the way we make use of our shells that reveals who we are.

BREATHE

Breathe. Breathe. BREATHE! Panic seizes me as yet again I am awakened by a muscle spasm that has sealed my windpipe shut. I frantically gulp for air, managing only to swallow great quantities of it and add to my discomfort. Fifteen seconds. Suzanne has heard my struggles and is rushing to elevate my head so I can try and relax my throat. Thirty seconds. I desperately strain for any wisp of new air in my lungs, sweat pouring from my body as if trying to make way for oxygen to enter directly through my skin. Forty-five seconds. How long before I lose consciousness? Should Suzanne dial 911? How would...I...even signal...her...to do...that? Sixty seconds.

A weak groan accompanies a small puff of air escaping my lungs, making room for fresh. Like sipping air through a pinhole. But the sip eases panic's grip, allowing purpose to gain hold over me. Force air out, sip air in. Struggle. Groan out, gasp in. Relax. Breathe in, breathe out, until purpose is blissfully rewarded with balance. And balance restores strength and peace.

Breathe in, breathe out. Take a deep breath in. The rush of oxygen is so gratifying, so nourishing for a healthy physical life. Yet we need nourishment for living, not just for life. How can we "breathe in" to nourish our daily lives and combat the suffocated panic too many of us feel? Fortunately, we have answers. Pray, worship, and study the Scripture or, more broadly, meditate, cultivate a humble and thankful life, and learn. These things help us tap in to our sources of strength, affirm our place in the world by not allowing us to either over- or understate our place and role in the universe, and give us knowledge and wisdom from the perspective and experience of others. We are planted...fed...allowed to root.

Breathe in, breathe out. Interesting how often we talk about breathing as simply breathing in. But what happens if we just hold air in? What was nourishment becomes stale, even suffocating. The initial sigh of refreshment becomes a scream for release. After all, the point of breathing isn't the taking in, but the exchange. What would our lives be if we did nothing but nourish ourselves? Our lives would suffocate, our newfound strength screaming for release. But we can allow our lives to breathe out through serving others, nurturing relationships, and giving. Through these actions, we share our strength and our plantedness to create a stronger, happier, and more just world. Our roots grow, bloom, and provide beauty and fruit for the world. And our lives make room for fresh nourishment.

Breathe in – pray, worship, and study. Breathe out – serve, accompany, and give. Unfortunately, breathing for life is much easier than breathing for living. But perhaps a small puff out – volunteering, spending time with someone in need, or donating to a worthy cause – will stem the suffocation in your life, allowing space for renewed purpose for breath to take root. Breathe in, breathe out until it becomes habit and purpose is blissfully rewarded with balance. And balance restores strength and peace.

OYSTERS

We are all meant to shine, as children do. We were born to make manifest the glory of God that is within us. It's not just in some of us; it's in everyone. And as we let our own light shine, we unconsciously give other people permission to do the same. As we are liberated from our own fear, our presence automatically liberates others."

Marianne Williamson

Ever hear of someone collecting oyster shells? Probably not. Let's be honest here. With their nondescript coloring, lumps, rough edges, and irregular shape, oysters are ugly. It is only when the shell opens that we can see the treasure within – a beautiful pearl. Although beautiful, the pearl gains value only when given away, and only when the pearl is gone does the oyster become free to grow another.

How often do we see ourselves as oysters – plain, rough, even downright ugly, leading a nondescript life devoid of any real value? But this view of ourselves is a lie. The truth is that within each of us grows a pearl of great price, a gift given us by the Creator. But until we are willing to risk opening our shells to give the pearl away, we will never realize how truly valuable we are, and we will never have the opportunity to grow a new one. Our pearl is a gift to give the world, making this a better place for all. The more we give of ourselves to others, the more capacity we develop for giving and the more valued we feel as individuals. And opening our shells to give is contagious – as we give, we grant permission to others to open their shells.

FORMATION

My mother worked as a Girl Scout camp nurse, so as a small child, summers found me packing up to go to Grandma and Grandpa's home in Madison, Wisconsin. The trip there was magical, for my grandpa drove the Greyhound bus that connected our two cities. I always sat right behind him, marveling at everything he did to get the huge bus, its passengers, and their luggage from town to town along the way. My job, self-appointed, was to make sure everyone on the bus knew that the driver was my grandpa. And I did my job well.

When we got to Madison, Vanessa was staying at my grandparents', too. Vanessa was a

couple years older than me, but every summer we had a great time going to the playground, visiting the zoo to ride the elephants and camels, and simply coloring and playing games in my grandparents' dark, damp, old basement. We sometimes even went to the five-and-dime store at the end of the block to get a soda or a new coloring book, but some people gave us odd looks.

Vanessa and I always went to Vacation Bible School at my grandparents' church because Grandma taught there. We played games, laughed, and sang songs. Grandma's favorite song, and therefore mine, went "Jesus loves the little children, all the children of the world. Red or yellow, black or white, they are precious in his sight. Jesus loves the little children of the world." I had no idea what that meant.

In 1969, when I was nine years old and watching Walter Cronkite with my father (we never watched the news, we watched Walter

Cronkite), I became really confused by a report on the unfolding race riots. My small-town, middle-class, white upbringing gave me no context for ideas like race, prejudice, oppression, or poverty. I suddenly became fearful and asked my dad, "Is Vanessa black?" "Of course," said my dad. "Vanessa's mom doesn't have a place for Vanessa to stay when Vanessa is not in school. Grandma takes Vanessa out of the projects each summer so her mom can keep her job."

My next visit with Vanessa was just as fun, but the looks at the five-and-dime suddenly felt sinister. And the bus ride home brought worries about what Vanessa would go home to.

I am forever grateful to my grandmother for giving me the pearl of knowing that all people are children of God, princes and princesses of the kingdom of God, and deserving of all the love, honor, and dignity that title confers. And I am grateful to my parents for raising me to recognize and avoid prejudice. Suzanne and I have tried to honor these gifts by giving our children opportunities to experience different people and ways of life. In turn, they have taught us more about tolerance, acceptance, and to not forget the truths all children know:

Every day begun with optimism brings wonder, joy, and friendship;

We all are equally gifted and valuable;

We all have the same basic needs for food, housing, safety, love, and fun;

We can all play together when we're kind to each other and agree on the rules; and

The only important label for anyone is "friend."

I split each summer trip between my two sets of grandparents. One of my earliest memories comes from an incident at the other grandparents' home. I was playing with an older neighbor boy who I looked up to, and I wanted him to like me.

He played baseball and wanted to practice his swing, but we had no ball. He suggested we swing at the bushes in front of my grandparents' house, and soon we had a lively imaginary baseball game going.

The game lasted until my grandmother came out to see what the racket was. She angrily sent the other boy home, and I realized how much damage we had done to those poor bushes. They were nearly destroyed, branches twisted every which way and raw wood glistening with sap visible everywhere. I knew I was in serious trouble.

My grandmother led me inside and got the story of what happened through my tears. At some point, my grandfather came home from working in his barbershop, fuming loudly, wanting to know what happened to the bushes. My grandmother took him aside and talked him out of his anger.

Instead of being punished, my grandmother forgave me and taught me year after year that I never had to do anything but be myself to have friends, the right kind of friends who liked me without me having to impress them. What wonderful gifts I got from her – forgiveness, grace, and a foundation of self-esteem that would serve me throughout life.

HORN BORN

Try googling "nerd" or "geek"; there must be a grade-school-era picture of me in one of the links. My mother often had to shoo me outside to play, or else my shyness and introversion would have kept me in my room by myself. I loved going to the library to get books and recordings of both music and short stories. A voracious reader, especially of classic adventure stories, I had flown through the Robert Louis Stevenson, Mark Twain, and Jack London pantheon – along with Gulliver's Travels and Moby Dick – by the end of fifth grade. In my spare time, I read the encyclopedia, A-Z. Told you – I'm a nerd. (And now I'm blessed with that never-ending rabbit hole called Wikipedia!).

As much as I loved (and continue to love) reading, I could never read and listen to music at the same time. For me, music can never be in the background. Even when my older sisters practiced their piano or flutes, I would stop whatever I was doing and listen. While reading took me places I had never been, music took me places that could never be except in my mind at that very moment. In music, I found pure creative exploration and emotion, unbound by words, physical space, or time. A means to unlock my mind and give voice to emotions that had no other language.

My parents started piano lessons for me in fifth grade, but I soon became impatient with my teacher for not giving me music I wanted to play, and piano fell by the wayside – temporarily. Before sixth grade, I wanted to play saxophone and tried to pick one up from school. The band director listened to my request, then gave me a horn (commonly, but erroneously, called French horn) to try instead. He was surprised I could get notes out of it and convinced me to take it home. He probably already had enough saxophone players and was looking for any sucker willing to try and tackle the (unbeknownst to me) devilishly difficult horn. Whatever the band director's motivation, I immediately fell in love with the instrument and played constantly. In the horn, this shy, socially awkward boy found an instrument with an incredible range of expression. And the horn is an instrument you don't merely hold. You hug a horn.

By high school, I was playing professional solo repertoire. I performed in school band and orchestra, brass and woodwind quintets, and civic orchestra, but even that wasn't enough. Horn had become the musical gateway drug. I started playing piano again, taught myself pipe organ, and became interested in early music by learning recorders. In my typical school day, I practiced horn or organ during lunch hour then, after dinner, played piano, horn, and recorders, read a while and then, if there was still time, looked at my homework.

During my senior year, I gave a public recital with a friend where I played horn, organ, and recorders, attended by perhaps 60 people. At the end I was emotionally spent and about to duck out when I saw real happiness in the audience members' faces. I had helped bring joy and beauty into these people's lives! This was, in so many ways, my opening night. The unassuming oyster had given the pearl away, and I desperately wanted to do it again.

Career guidance told me there was no money in music and I'd never pay off student loans or support a family, so I went to Valparaiso University to study chemistry and dabble in music. I quickly found myself dabbling in chemistry and studying music – scores, composition, playing horn 10 or more hours per day, and playing in an early music ensemble – so after one semester I became a music major in horn performance. I was still shy and introverted, but once a horn was in my hands, no challenge was too great, no audience was too large, and no solo was too nerve-wracking to attempt. By the time I graduated, I had spent four years as first chair of the horn section and had some proficiency on 40 different instruments – including saxophone.

MICHELLE AND I PLAYING RECORDERS

Unfortunately, I succumbed to career pressure before my senior year, graduating with a degree in German, then earning a Master of International Management and working for more than 25 years in finance and business strategy consulting. I never stopped playing my beloved horn, though most of the time it was in my living room and at church, and I taught horn as well as recorder in my free time to anyone interested.

COME SAIL AWAY

A love of sailing is one of the great pearls my father gave me. We spent many quiet hours together on sailboats, punctuated, as the saying goes, by moments of sheer terror. I liked sailing at the edge, heeling the boat over until it was easier to stand on the mast than on the deck. It was a great way to get to know each other and ourselves. My father says sailing is cheaper than a psychiatrist.

My sailing career got off to an extremely shaky start. Dad, a Navy veteran, had wanted a sailboat his entire life. Finally, in his early 40s and with me as a 15-year-old son, he had saved enough money to buy a 12-foot boat that we could sail in Wisconsin's many lakes. He towed it to our house on a Wednesday and gleefully made plans for the family to go to a lake that Saturday to try it out. In the meantime, he carefully stored the boat in the front of the garage with wheel chocks in front of the car tires to ensure no one pulled the car in too far.

On that Friday evening, I was left alone at home for several hours. It was a beautiful May evening, so I decided I was going to take the car, a stick shift Mustang, for a spin. Never mind that I had never driven a car and had no license; intellectually I knew how to do it. And, I reasoned, how different could it be from driving my rural friends' tractors anyway? I started the car, shifted into a gear I thought was reverse, gave it a little gas, and eased the clutch out a bit. Nothing happened, so I gave it more gas and less clutch. Still nothing. So with all the patience of a teenage boy, I really revved the engine and popped the clutch all the way out. Squeal, SLAM. The Mustang, actually in first gear, leapt over the wheel chocks and crashed into the sailboat, putting a 10-foot crack in the hull of my father's 12-foot dream. That I survived the night after my father came home proves there is a gracious God and that my father loves his children.

JOHN, CLAIRE AND I IN THE BOAT I NEARLY DESTROYED 30 YEARS EARLIER

I was grounded until I paid for the repairs (I washed floors and windows at an office supply store for $1.25 an hour), but we still had the boat in the water that summer. And so began a lifelong love of sailing.

Sailing is a unique lens through which to view life. While sailing, a person experiences first-hand the eternal paradox of water: calming and life-giving, yet chaotic and potentially life-destroying. Any given moment can be tranquil and rejuvenating, exhilarating, a test of all your physical, emotional, and intellectual capabilities, or it can be frightening. A sailor needs to make brutally honest assessments of whether a challenge is surmountable or if seeking shelter is the best decision. He or she cannot simply point the boat toward a destination and power through the elements to reach it, but must harness the wind and water, adjusting the sails and heading to create harmony with the environment even if headwinds dictate a slow zigzag toward the goal. Having friends along on the ride who know how to sail is a great help as all work together as a team, but even companions who know nothing about sailing can help balance the boat.

Life is a lot like that with unpredictable chaos and comforting calm – challenging, exhilarating, and requiring us to be fully present with all our being to make the most of our journey. We can't expect to define a goal and power straight at it. We need to work in harmony with everything around us and be open to the occasional zigzag when life blows straight into our faces. We need to be open and honest about our capabilities and limitations, and we need to recognize when seeking shelter and rest

DAD AND I IN HIS SECOND SAILBOAT

is the most prudent course. And while friends who share similar journeys can be especially helpful, friends who know nothing about what we are going through but are there to share the ride can still provide the balance critical to us reaching our destination.

We know many people who, after receiving a diagnosis of ALS, try to deny or hide this storm in their lives. Some have even chosen not to tell their children what was happening, leaving the family scared and bewildered when a loved one becomes paralyzed. To me, this is like a person in a small fishing boat getting caught in a raging storm, pounding against violent waves and winds. Forsaking the comfort, shelter, and support of a harbor full of family and friends in a futile attempt to power alone to an unreachable destination, these people have died bitter and lonely, with precious little peace for those left behind. There is a difference between fighting disease and fighting reality. Family, friends, faith, therapeutic devices, and medical therapies are not parts of the storm, they are tools at the ready when needed.

Suzanne and I have very intentionally chosen the sailboat option, harnessing the elements as we are able and charting a different course. We do what we can to raise money and awareness for ALS, to share our time and resources to help others navigate this disease, and, using the time freed up by not working, to better our community. We have also learned where our limits are and when we need to rely on the help and shelter of others.

Something's Wrong

In late November 2003, my extended family gathered at my parents' home. As was sometimes the case at such gatherings, those who wished would offer some musical entertainment.

Well, my children may remember it differently. As Michelle, our oldest, likes to say, they were probably voluntold to play or sing. Pardon my wife, Suzanne, and me for being proud of our children and having lofty expectations of them. We often voluntell our children to help at church or in the community and to share their gifts with others. Hopefully service and sharing will become lifelong habits for them.

When my turn came at our family gathering, I began playing Suite Bergamasque, a piano piece of some difficulty by Claude Debussy. Many people know of this piece because of its third movement, Clair de Lune. I had learned it in college in an attempt to impress Suzanne. It was technically well beyond me, but through force of will and hundreds of hours of practice, I twisted my largely self-taught hands into memorizing something Debussy might actually have recognized. What we do for women! Anyway, I was proud of being able to play it – precisely because my level of skill indicated I had no business even attempting it – and I loved the feeling I had while playing this gorgeous piece.

Halfway through the first movement on my parents' piano, my fingers stopped responding, as if I were nervous or had forgotten the notes. It had been decades since I'd been nervous while performing and, as I scanned the keyboard, my mind knew exactly what to do. My fingers were just like rebellious teenagers – no matter what I communicated, they weren't listening.

I gave up, frustrated, sad I couldn't finish, and quietly but deeply disturbed by uneasiness. Five years later, we would recognize this as the first indication of damage to my upper motor neurons. Thoughts and intentions were not being translated properly into signals to produce movement.

Fourth of Four

We all have become accustomed to hearing horn being featured in the music we hear. From *Star Wars* to *Pirates of the Caribbean*, from Sgt. *Pepper's Lonely Hearts Club Band* to *Tommy*, from *West Side Story* to Phantom of the Opera, the sound of the horn pervades our culture. When the music calls for something noble, triumphant, regal, mysterious, or romantic, the horn is the instrument of choice for modern composers. But it was not always so.

Horn was one of the last additions to what we would now consider the standard orchestra. Its origins are literally with animal horns blown as signals in the grazing field or during battle. As the horn evolved into a metal instrument, it was folded into one or more hoops so it could be slung over the shoulder, leaving one or both hands free while riding a horse or wielding a crook.

I can only imagine what the diva harpists, violinists, and flautists, accustomed to their ornate sanctuaries and courtly parlors, thought when told to make music with this unrefined tool of farm and field. Making matters worse are the noises that can come out of it. The horn is like a wild horse – even in the best of hands, it can't really be tamed. Just when you relax, thinking you and the horn have reached a good working relationship, it rears, bucks, bolts, and generally makes you sound incompetent. You can blame mistakes on the horse if you are in the field, but the concert hall offers no such refuge. Mozart called Josef Leutgeb, his horn-playing friend, an incompetent dumbass. He even composed a Musical Joke parodying all the mistakes made by horn players. To be fair, Mozart also composed four gorgeous horn concertos for Leutgeb and for all humanity. Even now, I must confess that one of my secret pleasures at the symphony is counting the missed notes coming out of the horn section. I'm not passing judgment, but commiserating and silently cementing my brotherhood with them. "Oh boy, have I ever done that before."

Bach, Handel, and Mozart tinkered with including two horns in orchestral works, writing passages that often imitated hunting horn calls. By the time Beethoven composed his Ninth Symphony, two horns were common, the music they were given was more varied, and composers including Haydn and Beethoven had experimented with writing for four horns in their symphonies. It is telling, though, that the third and fourth horns were given less demanding parts. The composers weren't stupid – they knew that finding four high-level horn players for a performance was far from certain, and they often doubled the first part with the third horn, allowing the best player to rest during easy sections and be less fatigued for the glamour or solo passages. And so, the fourth horn was basically given the impossible task of trying to not screw up the easiest part, becoming the target of jokes and derision – the last player of the least among instruments.

In the serene slow movement of his Ninth Symphony, Beethoven composed a solo passage for horn. Specifically for the fourth horn – the last of the least. And this is not the typical momentary step into the spotlight. The fourth horn is the only horn playing for seven minutes. Beethoven's Ninth remains the only piece I know where the conductor traditionally asks the last chair of a section to rise and be recognized with applause at its conclusion.

Beethoven was a fervent believer in Enlightenment ideals of replacing the ruling class structures and rules with liberty for and equality of all people. Reason, invention, and creativity were valued over birth station. Free will, rather than birthright, connected us and liberated all to find joy in a life path of each person's choosing.. He had a very emotional stake in these ideals, having been twice rejected for marriage by women of nobility because of his common birth. He never did marry.

The Ninth Symphony is a celebration of the brotherhood and sisterhood of all humanity, united as equals by free will without regard to class or social status and equally blessed by the

Creator with the gift of joy. Scholars debate the "what were you thinking, Herr Beethoven?" question of the fourth horn solo, but here's my opinion. Beethoven is simply practicing what he is preaching, um, composing, by uplifting the efforts and value of the last of the least. The fourth horn is an orchestral representation of our common humanity where we all struggle to

do our best with what we have been given, making plenty of mistakes along the way. We all celebrate joy and endure failure, and we all have value. Beethoven states plainly and for all to hear "you may be the fourth of four, but in my world your gift, your musical voice, is just as essential as everyone else's. I celebrate you, and I celebrate you lavishly."

What a gift of grace! After all, we are all the fourth of four at something. There is always that thing we need, want, or even love to do, but we simply aren't as good at it as others. We struggle to do our best, but make mistakes for all to see anyway. I was overcome for 25 years by the feeling of not being good enough, leading to round after round of deep depression. We all yearn for that joyous moment in our lives when someone plays the role of Beethoven in our lives, freeing us by saying "Who you are and what you do matters to me. Here's your opportunity and whatever your best is, it is good enough for me."

Of course, part of the transformative power of grace exemplified by Beethoven is the challenge in our own relationships with others. He was not known as a kind, sensitive soul, but as rude and even downright mean at times. Yet he found a way to share grace in other ways. It is all too easy to find fault with others when they make mistakes, to laugh at the work of others that may not meet our standards, or to deprive people of opportunities because we don't think they merit a shot at even a minor stint in the spotlight. The Ninth Symphony is a reminder for me to find who the fourth of four is in my world so I might uplift and celebrate them with a standing ovation. No matter what mistakes they've made. Encouragement is a pearl always ready to be given away.

LOVE

"To love another person is to see the face of God." Victor Hugo penned possibly the most powerful and life-changing line in secular literature when he wrote these words in *Les Miserables*. Why is this simple statement such a big deal? For millennia, people were taught that looking into the presence of God brought death. In the Hebrew Scriptures, Moses was told both at the burning bush and on Mount Sinai to turn away from God's presence, and the temple priests were instructed to go into the Holy of Holies on their hands and knees, backward. The depth of our unworthiness was simply too great to withstand the perfect holiness of God. We were warned that looking into the face of the perfect God could only result in death.

Then came Jesus, Emmanuel, God With Us, looking straight into our faces and saying "I know how broken you are but I love you as you are. I don't care who you are or what you've done. The way you are is enough and I deem you worthy of my love and deserving of all dignity and honor. Look at me, touch me, do what I do – love God and love each other."

But it is so hard to follow this command. We are afraid to be vulnerable, to open ourselves up to people in the way that loving them requires. And we have to be honest with ourselves; the reason we avoid the vulnerability of love is that we still believe either we or the other person is somehow, deep down, unworthy. We all have our dark secrets that stain our lives, the dirt we are loathe to show to anyone else. We all have moments where we view ourselves as somehow undeserving of love or in some way better than another, entitling us to withhold love from them. And so loving others becomes lost in the noise of life and is replaced by prideful, competitive behavior that seeks to stake out an area of self-worth defined by knowledge, status, or money. And we begin building shells around our area, separating us from each other and protecting what is "ours," including that dark stain.

But if God's love makes us worthy to face God, we can surely be bold to step outside our shells and feel worthy in the face of other people. God's love is a gift that sanctifies us, and, as we reflect that love to others, that stain is cleansed from our lives so we have nothing to fear. It is a gift we are commanded to share.

What can happen if, as Victor Hugo wrote, we begin to see the face of God in everyone as we love those around us? Would we jockey for social position or fall on our knees to hug their feet? If they were lonely, would you walk by or take time to talk? What would you do if they were hungry? Hurt? In need? What of that which you consider to be "yours" would you withhold when confronted with the face of God?

Love is another pearl you have been given. Share it with everyone you encounter and look for the face of God in each person. You will never be the same.

Relationship

Reflect for a moment on the best relationships in your life. Whether friends, family, or the love of your life, what exactly is it that makes those relationships work and grow through the years? Is it common interests and experiences, a harmonious compatibility one with the other? Or is something else at work in your cherished relationships?

Compatibility may bring people together but it will not keep us together. At some level, we have incompatibilities with all those with whom we share our lives, incompatibilities that come out through time, exposing and straining the frail sinews that bind us to each other. At these times it may be difficult to remember what brought you into relationship or to even recognize the person you thought you knew so well.

When the bonds of compatibility fail, when the love we have for someone is hard to find, we must make a choice. Is the love for that person, the value of that person in our life, worth the effort, pain, and sacrifice necessary to push this relationship through crisis and conflict? In other words, what level of commitment are we ready to bring to a relationship? Commitment is the key to every relationship, and it is the bottom-line responsibility we cannot shirk if we are to live a healthy life in community with others. A relationship founded in love and buttressed by commitment becomes a sanctuary, an unassailable refuge from strife within and without.

Suzanne is a beautiful example of a person choosing to sacrifice and commit to a loving marriage relationship. Many spouses choose divorce when confronted with the overwhelming, exhausting enormity of effort required to care for someone with ALS, and we must be careful not to judge these people harshly. Suzanne, driven by commitment and love, has chosen the hard path, the near invisible journey along a road horrifically pitted with obstacles and sacrifice. It has been many years since midnight feedings and diaper changes for our children, yet in caring for me, Suzanne must still wake in the middle of every night to roll me over. She must get me out of bed; bathe, dress and feed me; administer my medicines and breathing treatments; drive me everywhere I need or want to go; change my diapers; and get me back in bed at night. Nursing would have been her absolute last career choice, yet Suzanne gave up her job to attend to my care. We have revised every plan, every dream we had for this time in our lives, and we struggle to carve out any small, short section of path that might recall a normal married relationship. We get angry, tired, and frustrated, but the refuge of our relationship provides a blessed sanctuary wherein strife can be met with grace, forgiveness, and peace, and Suzanne's love and commitment blaze anew with the break of every day.

In all of these ways, Suzanne is a daily reminder of the ministry of Jesus. His commitment to be in relationship with us led Him to choose the hard path and make the ultimate sacrifice. I experience grace and peace within the refuge of God's relationship with me, and I look forward to every new day to experience the love borne out of Jesus' commitment to the relationship between Suzanne and me.

Please take care to grow and share pearls of commitment. Your world and the lives of those around you will be better able to deal with the rough places, and love will bloom anew each day.

GIVING, UPSIDE-DOWN

Rugged individualism. The self-made man (or woman). Individual liberty. These are such strong archetypes in our culture, attributes we are taught to admire and include in our aspirations. Needing people, needing help, is so often perceived as a weakness to be hidden and kept private. However, I believe these cultural messages are unbiblical and unhealthy to us as individuals and as a society.

Jacob, Moses, and David all called out to God, recognizing their inability to live lives blessed by God on their own merits. In the New Testament, those who called out in faith to Jesus are those who received healing and spiritual life. Time after time, God reminds us to care for the poor, sick, widowed, and foreign in our communities. The Bible teaches us to be in relationship with each other not simply for friendship but to care for, support, and uplift all who are in our midst.

We have witnessed all too often the results of people not reaching out for help. Suicides, violent outbursts, lives broken by bullying and abuse are so rampant only the particularly sensational reach the public consciousness. Worse, the malaise is so common the general population has come to accept a certain level of hurtful dysfunction. Even the worst, most heinous crimes fade from the national conversation in a short time with nothing changed to lessen the likelihood of a similar incident in the future. "He was a quiet, nice boy," we say. "We had no idea she felt so hurt, so worthless," we cry. "If only we had known she needed help."

If only we knew. If only we knew, we would have been there for them. We would have made sure he got the help he needed. We would have driven her to her appointment, bought him some groceries, and paid her doctor bill. After all, we love helping those in need. We feel good about doing good for others.

But we didn't know, often because we as individuals and as a society don't teach people to reach out and ask for help. Even though we know the joy and fulfillment we receive in helping others, we don't teach people in need that it is okay to ask for help. Think about how twisted that is. How can we experience that joy of giving if no one asks to receive help?

We must recognize the need to teach people, starting with our family and friends, to give the gift of asking for help. It is not a weakness; it provides an opportunity for others to give of themselves and create stronger community bonds. The gift of asking for help when there is a need connects us, strengthens us, and lifts us all.

Choices

The phone rings, and Matthew turns it to speaker and positions it where I can use it. On the other end is a man from New Jersey who tells me I have no time to lose. For $7000 I could purchase his meditation and visualization program to cure my ALS. He goes on to describe how he has totally healed several people with ALS. "That's amazing!" I said. "You must have gotten some tremendous press from such success. Why don't you send me some case study documentation, press coverage, or references before I make a decision?" He promises to send me information but never asks for a postal address (I didn't offer one), and he hangs up hurriedly. As it turned out, this man had tried swindling several other people.

While this is an extreme and obvious case, every challenge in life involves making choices. The fewer conventional answers that exist, the more effort you need to put forth to understand your situation medically, socially, emotionally, and spiritually. ALS has exactly zero conventional answers, so there are an enormous number of decisions to make. I found that taking control over my situation turned my personal narrative away from what life is doing to me and toward what I am doing for life. The worst thing I can do is allow myself the selfish conceit of victimhood. Being a victim does nothing to improve the situation and closes one's shell into the ugly oyster no one wants.

But claiming control must be a balance between doing nothing and trying everything. Making uninformed decisions out of desperation is not the same as taking control. The Food and Drug Administration doesn't hold a monopoly on medical wisdom, but that doesn't mean every wingnut selling something on the internet deserves anyone's time or money.

Buoys

Food, water, air and shelter are necessities to keep us alive, much like many land animals. But we are so much more complex than that. We need dignity, acceptance, inclusion, peace, affirmation, and purpose in order to live any kind of fulfilled life. Without them life feels like a constant struggle to keep our heads above water while being dragged under water by so many chains.

Our society is seemingly overrun with chains. The messages we see and hear too often come with more links in the chains that bind and weigh down our spirits. "You're not good enough." Clink goes another length of chain as it gets added to the burden you already struggle against. "Have you thought about dieting or going to the gym?" Clink. "Why don't you have a boy/girlfriend?" Clink. "If you were more successful you could get that new home, car, more stuff or even a more attractive partner." "If you fall behind you're a failure." "Be afraid, all that stuff you have could be taken away in an instant." "You're different, you don't fit in." "Look at that poor man in the wheelchair." Clink, clink, clink. When will it ever end?

We have all been given the ultimate gift to set us free from every chain and burden we could ever face. It comes to us freely, we don't have to earn it or do anything to deserve it, and it never fails or runs out. This gift is God's grace. Grace doesn't see ugly, only beautiful. Grace knows you and accepts, even rejoices in, who you are. Grace looks past every failure and holds us all in abundant love and inestimable, equal, worth.

What should we do with this amazing, life-changing gift? We could use it to simply slip our chains and head to shore. But what if we fashioned that grace into a buoy, using our old chains to anchor it? Our buoy could be a guide, lighting the way through life's difficult waters for others to help others navigate safely, securely, through. You can uplift the lives and spirits of those around you by being quick to forgive, releasing others from your expectations, refusing to gossip, including without preconditions, listening without judgment, and affirming the value and beauty of every life. Abundantly sharing the life-sustaining grace we have been given brings us a purpose that society's burdensome messages never can.

DIAGNOSIS, ACT I

Lying on an examination table, I try to force an out-of-body experience in order to keep my mind off of the knitting needle-sized probes stuck deep in my arm by the first neurologist I have seen. I hate needles and have been known to pass out during blood draws. The neurologist is trying to find out why the muscles in my right arm are twitching.

It is June 2004, and I am here on the advice of my primary care physician because the arm has been twitching since March. Nonstop, even at night. It's nothing big, just a quiver in the muscles much like people often get in an eyelid. It doesn't hurt; it's just odd and annoying. (And a little bit humorous – at more than one family dinner over the years, my dancing muscles have provided the mealtime entertainment. If only I had a tattoo.

Earlier tests ruled out multiple sclerosis and Parkinson's disease, and my primary care physician has never seen anything like this before. Here, my family and I are introduced to the rabbit's hole that is neurological medicine, where there are often more questions than answers, few definitive tests, and where our limited understanding of the workings of our bodies is most exposed.

When the examination is over I sit up, noting the exam table is literally pooled with sweat. The doctor says he needs more time to study the results, but I ask what the possibilities are. He lists carpal tunnel syndrome, heavy metal poisoning, multifocal motor neuropathy, post-polio syndrome, and a number of other ailments large and small. He mentions ALS but notes that, at 44, I am too young for it (actually untrue – ALS can strike people from their teens into their senior years and a relatively large percentage see disease onset while in their 40s) and that there is no sign of upper motor neuron involvement. It would be years before we connect the piano-playing incident with my disease.

During the period before my follow-up appointment, I become the poster child for internet-based hypochondria, frantically researching neurological disorders and reaching a new conclusion on my disease at least twice per day. At the appointment, the neurologist says I likely have benign fasciculation syndrome, a term used by doctors when they have no idea why the muscles fasciculate, or twitch, and he thinks it is harmless. I go happily on my way and give Suzanne the good news. Another doctor visit a month later finds nothing new, so he is convinced there is nothing to worry about. We are incredibly relieved.

TEMPEST

"In the depths of winter, I finally learned there was in me an invincible summer."

Albert Camus

The maelstroms of life are always with us. They might be over the horizon, out of sight for the moment, or you might be enveloped by one and being sucked down ever further into its vortex. Some maelstroms are literal, such as tsunamis, hurricanes and tornadoes, while others are metaphorical, like illness or distressed relationships and finances. We will never be able to avoid all of them as we travel through life.

Experienced sailors know what gear to pack in case of foul conditions , plan their voyage to avoid known and unnecessary risks, and how to pick and train crew to handle a boat through difficulties. We can take their example and apply it by planning well, building strong, supportive relationships , ceaselessly learning about ourselves and our world, and strengthening our faith to recognize and call on the power of God in our lives. If we do these things we will be able to navigate around or through most storms we encounter.

We all will encounter a maelstrom we cannot get through. Mine is probably ALS; barring a miracle, a medical breakthrough, or some other fatal situation, the vessel of my life will be crushed in the vortex of ALS. When that happens, I am grateful to know that God will lift me out of the maelstrom and set me beside the river of life where no storm or anguish exists.

DIAGNOSIS, ACT II

In July 2005, I dropped a glass platter in the sink while doing dishes, breaking it. Weakness and cramping in one hand forced me to go to a different neurologist. My wife came with me in case the doctor wanted to probe me with more needles. (I didn't want to go through that alone again). After doing only muscle strength/coordination tests and a reflex test (which turned out negative) and upon looking at my hands, he said "You have ALS." Then he pulled out the needles for my arms and legs. Neurologists can be particularly sadistic. At least, the bad ones.

After the test, the neurologist brought us from the exam room into his office, where the rest of the conversation went like this (I had done quite a bit of research prior to this appointment):

"Could this be Lyme Disease?"

"No."

"Multiple sclerosis?"

"No."

"Multifocal motor neuropathy or primary lateral sclerosis?"

"No."

"Heavy metal poisoning?"

"No."

"Spinal Muscular Atrophy or Kennedy's Syndrome?"

"No."

"Would diet changes help?"

"No."

"What about exercise?"

"Look. You are dying. You have three years, two if you're unlucky. Go home and call me when you need a wheelchair."

With those words the doctor finally put an end to my questions. Suzanne and I were crushed. We drove home in a total stupor, oblivious to the beautiful summer day, collapsed into bed, and sobbed.

Fortunately, all of our children were away at one camp or another for the week so we had some time to pray, talk, and generally get our heads right. Part of that process included going to see Wedding Crashers, a funny, mindless movie escape. I even convinced the normally arrow-straight Suzanne to smuggle in water bottles filled with straight-up kamikazes, a ferocious alcoholic concoction worthy of its name. Don't ask me how the movie ends.

During this week, we were given the strength to see three important things. First, contrary to the neurologist's opinion, I was living, not dying, and it made no sense to waste any of whatever time I had left in bitterness, fear, or self-pity. Time was precious, and there was much I could still do to positively impact the world around me. There was absolutely no point in sacrificing opportunities of the present to worry in anxiety about the future. In any case, we realized that none of us ever knows how much time we have. The second thing was that this neurologist was a jerk! I needed to take control of my own medical care, learn as much as I could, and get a second opinion from an ALS clinic. Third, we would refuse to become victims of this disease. We would not let it define us, and we would focus always on what we could do, not on what we could not do. All of us have "stuff" that life throws in our path and, if nothing else, there was much I could teach my children through this experience. Life is always worth maximizing, worth finding ways to make it count. And all the more so for being able to open my eyes each morning and see Suzanne's smile.

HORN MOURNED

From an email I sent on Tuesday, Dec. 12, 2006, 9:35 am:

I tried playing my horn a few weeks ago for the first time in a couple of months. My embouchure was a little out of shape, expectedly, but my breath support was fine. However, I couldn't keep my fingers on the valve keys or keep the keys held down for any length of time due to the misshapenness and weakness in my left hand. This keeps me from being able to play as I currently know how.

The feeling I had was not one of a hole being created in my soul – that would be too clean and neat – or even a rending of my soul. This was a complete shattering of my being. In many ways I think and feel not through, but in, music. For more than 35 years, playing horn has been my emotional voice, the best way for me to express who I am to the rest of the world.

Playing horn taught me that true Beauty is not found in what is seen (music on the page), but in what is experienced (music brought to life through performance), and that finding beauty in experience demands that you work at it – it won't simply appear to you. Playing horn also taught me that beauty does not demand perfection. In fact, it taught me that if you hope to approach perfection you must be willing to risk abject public failure and that we develop bonds with others more through our imperfections than through those things we do especially well. Timidity gets you nowhere, and there is a form of beauty in the failure resulting from a bold attempt.

When I would approach perfection, I experienced a dissolving of the physical world around me. The instrument, notes, director, orchestra, and any sensation of the mechanics of producing music simply ceased to exist; there was only pure beauty and joy around, in and through me, becoming my very breath. In this, my horn has also been a window, giving me a glimpse into something that can only be heaven.

And so I am currently wounded beyond anything I have ever experienced – more than my depression, my unemployment, or even the physical disease currently eating at my body.

And yet I find even these wounds to be healing. Healing is coming through hearing my children perform, seeing Suzanne grow in her appreciation of and even emotional reliance on music, hearing how other people I've taught are growing in their musicianship, and recognizing God is multiplying the gifts he gave to me.

Healing came when, during Michelle's most recent Valparaiso University concert where she played horn in the very spot I played during the peak of my technical abilities, one of my very favorite pieces and one I performed exceptionally well was on the program – a seldom-heard piece titled "Salvation is Created" by the almost unknown composer Pavel Tchesnokov. This cannot be coincidence. It reminded me that Advent is a time of awaiting the coming of Christ and that God not only can heal such a wound as I have, but He also knows my pain because He came to earth specifically to bear my sin and all of my wounds so that I certainly will be healed.

And Suzanne, whom God gave me as His arms and voice to comfort me and give me strength, has reminded me that waiting is not a passive thing – I need to prepare myself by using God's gifts to the best ability I have for his glory. She asked if there is some other way I can play, and indeed there is. Virtually all horn music written up through 1860 (and even many pieces after that) was written for horns without valves, so I'll be exploring the now-rare art of how to play natural (valveless) horn.

I don't know if I'll be successful doing this or, if I am, for how long, but I know I must make that bold attempt. I must because a horn player is who I am. I must because when God permanently heals all of my wounds and brings me to heaven (hopefully in 40 years!), I know God will not bother showing me a place in any "mansion with many rooms." I know God is going to show me to my chair in the horn section!

TRIALS AND TRIBULATIONS

"Are there any drug trials you could get into?" is one of the most frequent questions I hear. My normal response is "not at this time," but the reality is far more complex than such a short reply can begin to explain.

At any given time there are approximately 35,000 people living with ALS in the United States, with perhaps another 10 times that number in the rest of the world. While 350,000 to 400,000 people with ALS (pALS) might sound like a lot of folks, in the world of pharmaceutical markets that is a tiny number. So tiny that large pharmaceutical companies won't allocate resources to research potential drug therapies. We pALS simply don't represent a market worth pursuing. For a sense of scale, 55 million Americans are eligible for statin drugs. There is more money spent advertising erectile dysfunction medication than is spent on ALS research. And yes, pALS do feel screwed.

Of course, there are other research organizations beyond big pharma. Small drug companies will do research in niche areas like ALS where they don't have to compete with the giants, often in hopes of finding patentable medicines they can sell or license. There are also several independent laboratories such as those supported by the Les Turner ALS Foundation, ALS Therapy Development Institute and Project ALS. The government, through the National institutes of Health, also provides grant money to research conducted by pharmaceutical firms, universities, and independent laboratories. Additionally, the federal government classifies

ALS as an "orphan" (i.e. rare) disease, which can provide assistance to small pharma companies in the form of subsidies, enhanced patent protection, or streamlined FDA approval.

These research organizations are doing some tremendous work. We have learned more about this disease in the past 10 years than we did in the previous 150. The Ice Bucket Challenge rage of 2014 injected an enormous amount of money into the research space that, if well-managed, may prove the tipping point in cracking the codes for building truly effective therapies. Yet there are weaknesses in this system. Too often these organizations do not collaborate or communicate, especially with research trials outside of the United States. It is so frustrating to hear of precious resources being used to study questions already answered elsewhere. Also, the NIH mission was modified in 2002 to prioritize grants toward marketable product development so that the government can share in any profits. This has resulted in less money being available for basic research into, for example, how motor neurons in the brain function.

All of this results in a very small number of clinical trials starting up in a year. Compounding that problem is the set of criteria a patient needs to meet in order for a person to be accepted into a trial. A patient typically needs to be diagnosed between two and four years prior to the trial with a disease progression that falls within the "normal" bell curve, which automatically leaves out half of the patient population. Then patients have to be able to travel to the clinic, potentially leaving work or children and enduring great physical duress Even if a person can clear those obstacles, he or she might get a placebo for all his or her efforts. Personally, I never qualified for a trial. In the beginning, I wasn't sick enough and by the time I was, I'd been sick too long.

The few trials that do move forward try to fill 20-50 spots, a very small number for statistical significance, especially if only 15-30 are getting the real drug. The majority of pALS know this and will often go around the system. For example, about 10 years ago there was a trial for CoQ10 that took years to fill up the 50 spots. Many wondered why they should join the trial and risk getting the placebo when they could just run to Walgreen's and buy the stuff? With prescription drugs, people go to other doctors to get off-label prescriptions, so the problem with the CoQ10 trial also happened to the cretonne, l-arginine, ceftriexone, and minocycline trials. We can't do science that way.

A powerful example of patients taking control of our own research happened in 2008 after a small clinical trial in Italy suggested that Lithium Carbonate, often prescribed for bipolar disorder, might slow or even stop the progression of ALS. Online patient communities gained access to the study documentation and translated the Italian into English. We contacted the lead investigator to ask him more questions and began pushing U.S. organizations to begin a second, larger trial.

Roadblocks appeared immediately. We learned that trials needed to be approved by internal review boards charged with allocating staff time and research budgets and, critically, protecting the image and interests of the organization. Since Lithium Carbonate was a generic medicine, no pharmaceutical firm would profit and, therefore, none were interested in sponsoring a trial. Any funding for research would have to come from either the federal government, academic, or nonprofit sources, and it could take years to prioritize the resources.

This was clearly not acceptable to the community of pALS, so we decided to do our own trial. The Lithium trial started out with individuals getting off-label prescriptions from their doctors. We organized emails between people and we recorded our own results based on a standard ALS functional rating scale. We quickly had more than 80 people in the trial, the largest ALS trial in years. Disease progression was published on a Google doc for the first few months until an established ALS online community called Patients Like Me took on the data collection and analysis. Patients Like Me had, and continues to have, a broad reach of people across the globe along with a large database of disease progression in thousands of pALS. They also had the science credibility and publication access our initial little group lacked. Participation in this patient-led trial increased to more than 200. Within eight months, Patients Like Me published scientifically robust findings by comparing trial participant results to their history data. Well before traditional trials got underway, Patients Like Me published the conclusion that Lithium had no effect on disease progression.

Upon hearing these results, the medical establishment yawned. The general reaction was that this trial was flawed since patients reported their own data and there was no placebo control group. My response? I have never seen my neurologist following me around during the day to record if I can help my caregivers get me dressed or if I struggle for breath when I move or talk, examples of the standard functional rating scale questions. In other words, since I report my own results when I go into the clinic, why would my data be considered unreliable if I reported it to a website? Besides, what incentive did any of us have for lying about our condition? Also, I believe the statistical validity of using a historical record of thousands of people is greater than a placebo control group of 10. Patients Like Me was able to reach more people, collect data easier, and do better analysis with their extensive history base. They also were able to get more press attention. I continue to push for more widespread use of some of the concepts in that trial, especially comparing participant data to history databases instead of a placebo group. The patient-led Lithium trial was a testament to the power of community.

Unfortunately, the powerful drive of pALS to find a way to extend their lives attracts scum who would prey on the desperation of others. There are several examples of "stem cell" treatment centers across the globe that convince people to spend tens of thousands of dollars for treatments that do nothing. I once received a tip from a well-meaning person about a doctor having success with stem cell treatments. My email request for more information elicited the response that I would have to pay $500 to get on the waiting list for a $500 consultation and $5000 would be due at that time as a down payment for treatment. After doing some more research on this doctor, I could not find a single example of someone who was helped by him. Further, there was nothing in his background to suggest he had any education or experience in cultivating stem cells or turning stem cells into motor neuron cells. The handful of pALS I know who sought out this "treatment" felt well for a couple of months, then declined and died very quickly thereafter. Bogus stem cell treatment clinics have sprouted up in China, Israel, Thailand, Mexico, and Barbados.

Dozens of people sell "treatments" that include a bewildering array of machines, exotic plants, bath additives, dietary regimens, and supplements. One person found me in a newspaper article, used the internet to look up my phone number, and tried to convince me he could eliminate my ALS by improving my attitude through his "proven life coach" services. I told him the only negative attitude I had was about his quackery, and I would turn that into a positive by reporting him to the New Jersey Attorney General.

ot that I am against non-establishment therapies. I did acupuncture and some Chinese medicine and massage shortly after my diagnosis, and I felt good after those visits for a while. Neither the doctor nor Suzanne nor I were under any illusion this would cure me, and I stopped going when I no longer felt any benefit.

What is missing from all of these alternative treatments is evidence. People will jump up and down with religious fervor that they have found the answer to beating ALS and that the medical establishment is hiding the truth from us. They offer any number of improvable anecdotes and testimonials but no data. Those of us who have been around a while have seen many new, potential treatments come and go from establishment and alternative medicine sources alike. We have heard shouts of promise turn into grumbles of disappointment too many times to not be skeptical, and we have watched too many friends pouring out too much money chasing hope in phantoms. What we need is data, not anecdotes. Anyone considering an alternative treatment for any disease please, please demand evidence, weigh the risks both to your health and your finances, and research the background of everyone to whom you entrust your medical care.

A Pain In The ALS

I need to set something straight. There is a widespread view in the general medical community and public, perpetuated by out-of-date printed information, that ALS causes no pain. Any person who has ALS will beg to differ.

As the muscles weaken, they are no longer able to support the skeleton as they should, causing chronic pain in the neck (trying to hold up the giant melon), back, hips, and other joints. Arms come out of the shoulder joints all too easily, and even minor off-balance movements can seriously strain already-weakened back muscles. I have even had terrible pain in my transmandibular (jaw) joint caused by the stresses of an odd side effect of ALS – excessive yawning. Yawning also sometimes causes muscle cramps under the chin or in the tongue as a "special" bonus to the bone-crushing cramps in the legs.

An effect of upper motor neuron loss is muscle spasticity or stiffness. This is a major problem for me if I get cold or when I am stressed. The muscles refuse to allow the joints to bend, even with someone else pushing on my arms or legs. To me, it feels like the muscles, instead of stretching, are splintering like bent plywood. And inactivity can cause joints to lock.

None of this pain compares to that experienced by people with end-stage cancer. But in caring for a person with ALS, pain management needs to be in the conversation.

FINDING MY VOICE

After my 2005 diagnosis, Suzanne and I spoke about ALS and our journey to many churches, civic groups, and schools. We even journeyed with representatives from the Les Turner ALS Foundation to lobby state lawmakers about legislation to fund needed patient services. I was pleased that our legislators took the time to listen to me.

It is 2013. For each of the past four years I have been convinced that that year would be the one I would finally need to resort to using a computer voice. Each of the preceding years had come and gone with my voice becoming weaker and my tongue more paralyzed and atrophied, but my words remained intelligible in progressively more quiet settings. That is no longer true.

Every person with ALS faces decisions of when to stop independently doing normal adult activities like driving, walking, toileting or eating. These are all difficult losses physically and emotionally, and the decision process can be heart-rending. Driving, for me, was relatively easy. When I knew I would have difficulty reacting to an unforeseen situation, I gave my keys to Suzanne and never looked back. Likewise, I had few difficulties giving up normal food although the sight and smell of theater popcorn or a well-prepared meal sure is tantalizing. Giving up independent toileting was extremely difficult emotionally, especially whenever we had to ask my sons to help. John and Matthew have been nothing but gracious and respectful of this abhorrent task over the years.

I admit to being incredibly stubborn when it came to recognizing when to get off my feet and into a wheelchair. I resisted losing this perceived independence even after a year of walking only when someone held my arm, more than a dozen major falls, a couple of ambulance rides, and two concussions. Suzanne finally made me understand that the whole family was anxious every time I walked, that it was unfair to others to make them responsible for keeping me upright, and that I would have truer independence in a wheelchair. As always, she was right. All of these are losses that we grieve and, with the support of faith, family, and community, eventually move past.

For some reason, accepting that I need mechanical help to speak has been far more difficult for me than dealing with the loss of any of these other activities of daily living. Maybe it's because these speech generating devices slow down the conversation and significantly reduce spontaneity as one laboriously picks letters on an on-screen keyboard and then selects the "speak" button. There's nothing quite like adding to a conversation five minutes after it's over. The machines seriously ruin comedic timing! Perhaps it's because the computerized voices are the butt of so many jokes. Or maybe I simply dread the added isolation and impersonalization of putting a machine physically in front of me, into the middle of my conversation, and losing that individual identity connection to my unique voice. (Suzanne even keeps my old cell phone line active so she can occasionally listen to my voice mail greeting). On the other hand, it was really frustrating to spend enormous amounts of energy repeating myself and seeing the look in the eyes of people who are politely smiling and nodding because they don't want to tell me they can't understand me.

As we had with all of these major decisions, Suzanne and I reached out to our children to get their input and hear their feelings. As usual, their perception and discernment went beyond expectation and illuminated my path in areas I didn't dare stop and face. John commented on how he noticed me choosing words I could speak rather than what I would like to say, limiting the impact my conversations could have. All of the children reminded me that treating the device as a tool to be used when needed would help maintain and strengthen active relationships and actually enrich our lives.

So, with support and grace from Suzanne and our children, I began the search to determine which of the ridiculously high-priced devices was most appropriate for my needs. Through this search, I was once again struck by how different my ALS journey is compared to other Americans with the disease. My employer's group health insurance policy didn't cover these devices at all while Medicare would cover 80% of the cost.Though that would potentially leave a bill of $2000 - $3000 (without Medicare supplemental insurance), it was far better than paying the full cost which was close to $20,000. ALS doesn't respect financial resources and neither do our corporations or governments. What irks me even more is that anyone can buy a tablet and outfit it with eye tracking hardware and software for about $2500, but no private or public insurer will provide coverage for such a solution because tablets are not dedicated medical devices. The official excuse for such ridiculousness is that insurers are worried doctors all over the country will write thousands of fraudulent prescriptions for patients to get free tablets. I don't buy that excuse for a second. I trust doctors more than that. Besides, even if three of four prescriptions were fraudulent, insurers would still pay less than they do today buying dedicated speech synthesizers. I blame the durable medical equipment lobby.

While trying to reconcile the emotional and financial implications of this decision and as my speech deteriorated beyond intelligibility, I continued working as a consultant because of the dignity I found in work and in serving as an advocate for and example of diversity in the workplace. For nearly two years, I became functionally mute since there was no insurance coverage for a speech synthesizer. My family and caregiver became my translators as the amount of effort it took to get syllables out in one breath became exhausting. My isolation grew when I quit working and dropped out of mentoring high schoolers at church and abandoned other community service roles in which I had been active for more than a decade. But, with Medicare coverage in place of private medical insurance, I could finally order my speech generating device. When Claire left for college, Suzanne and I spent many nights sitting in silence at home, and we looked forward to the arrival of the device more than ever.

After an almost torturous wait of seven months, I finally got my speech machine and, when it arrived, I felt like I was crawling out of a dark cave. Suzanne began warning people that

I'd been saving up a lot of thoughts, so they'd better be ready for just about anything! One friend mentioned to Suzanne that she was looking forward to having a conversation with me, and we both realized we have dozens of friends who have never really heard who I am through conversation.

Once the device arrived, I had to decide which of the five to 10 male voices to claim as my own. The options all sounded so clinical and uninspiring – Mike16, Bob2 and the like. Why can't we choose from Sea Captain, President, Shakespeare, Preacher or maybe Lounge Lizard or Pirate? Hollywood is missing a new revenue stream in licensed voices. I would like a James Earl Jones, please. If he's not available, how about a Barry White or Ian McKellon? For those with a way back machine, I'd be happy with a Paul Robeson, too. I asked Suzanne which celebrity voice she would prefer, assuming she would pick Cary Grant, her favorite actor. She surprised me by choosing Vincent Price or Patrick Stewart. It seems that bass voices are the common denominator for choices in this family. Of course, all available voices are tenors. Sigh. Since these electronic voices can't emote, I could envision licensing several voices – maybe use the James Earl Jones for normal conversation, switch to a Don Rickles or a Gilbert Gotfried when I'm perturbed, and then pull out the Barry White to sweet-talk Suzanne.

The voice I chose is neither romantic nor Hollywood-esque; it is mechanical and not my own. The machine's pronunciations aren't always accurate. Conversations are slow and I'm often a topic behind. But, through all of this, the people who surround me gently persuaded me that my voice is more about what I say rather than how I sound, that my identity rings more clearly through what comes out from inside my character than in the machine that makes speech possible. My individual voice is still a loss all of my family grieves, but I am beginning to accept that I can make a difference in my world in a different way, finding a voice to spread love, comfort, peace, and grace to those around me. May God grant me empathy, wisdom, and patience.

Earth, Sea, and Sky

Where are you going and what are you doing today? Whether getting to work or school, running errands, doing chores, visiting, serving, or recreating, what kind of storms might you encounter? Are you prepared to weather them?

Earth, sea, and sky are three places to visit every day that can help you develop the strength, resources, and focus necessary to cope with any buffeting the day can bring. Earth is our ground, our habitat, our shared home. It is where we are sustained and connected, the place where we are created to be. Here we feel fed, restored, and grounded. We grow on earth even as we plant and nurture. Take time every day to till and weed the soil of your earth by tending to your family, faith, environment, connections, and communities even as you tend to those things that keep you healthy and growing.

The sea is a place of mystery, adventure, chaos, and passion. An unbroken horizon breathes of limitless possibility. Embarking on a voyage brings some level of uncertainty and expectation, perhaps even discomfort, yet the lure of the sea lights our imagination and expands our sense of the possible. We need the groundedness of earth, but without the metaphorical sea we are in danger of stagnation and limiting our understanding of where we can go and who we can become. We need to set sail into the unknown and even the uncomfortable to explore and discover new passions and possibilities.

But earth and even sea limit our vision to what and who are around us at any given moment. Launching into the sky dramatically expands our view. Being in the sky reveals where and how others live; it shows the condition of our earth and sea beyond our daily existence. Flight brings us together more quickly, through greater distances, than we can otherwise achieve. We can hear the stories of the other even as we are amazed at the beauty and variety of life. We experience beyond ourselves.

Find and till your earth, explore the seas of your possibility, and take to the sky to include others in your view each day. In so doing, you will meet and traverse the storms you find in this day with strength and peace.

RISE

In both the Hebrew Scriptures and the Christian Bible, there are many references to instances of miraculous physical healing. In many of these accounts, God simply tells the healed person (or his messenger) to rise or get up or go on his way.

Since I developed ALS, I have often thought about these people who were healed. How would a lame man have felt if, after a lifetime of begging at a corner, some rabbi walked by and said "Rise!"? What would I do if some stranger came up to me in my power wheelchair and told me to get up? Would I try to stand or would I give the (in my mind) idiot an annoyed look and go on my way? In thinking about this, I realized that when Jesus said "Rise," he was not issuing a command. He was offering an invitation – an invitation to a better life. An invitation that those who were healed accepted in faith.

And, truth be told, I now have a better life than before ALS. I am happier because I am focused on those things that are truly important, like loving my family, connecting with others, and trying to make the world around me a more just and caring place. I simply don't have time to worry about the outrageously trivial things that used to bog down my life, like whether or not I had the right job title, how much of a raise I "deserved," what stuff I " had" to buy next, or whether the person in front of me was driving fast enough. I have accepted Christ's invitation to a better life.

Do I pray for physical healing? Absolutely. But I also realize that any physical healing I might receive would only last maybe 20 or 30 years, while what God has done in my heart will last forever. So I never pray for physical healing without first thanking God for the amazing gift of healing already done in my spirit.

KICKING THE BUCKET LIST

"Needs better organizational skills." That phrase has probably shown up on every report card and performance review I ever received. Thank goodness I no longer work so I don't have to come up with another lame, lying answer for how I will improve myself in this area. It's just never going to happen. Planners, personal digital assistants, computer software, and sticky notes all failed to coerce or shame me into tidy, efficient organization. Some attempts survived a few weeks, most flamed out within a day or two. The problem all of these tools had was that at their black, rotted core stood a list.

"List" is the most vulgar, vile, four-letter spew of profanity. "List" is a tyrant, oppressing spontaneity and repressing possibility. "List" is the enemy of liberty, mandating what must be done while restricting what might be done.

So, what is on my bucket list? Perish *that* tortured thought. What would happen if I should die before all the items are checked off? Do I leave this world with a poor performance review for not meeting my goals? Or, what happens if I cross off that last item? Am I an underachiever for setting goals that are insufficiently lofty, and do I need to then make another (gag) list? The alternative is to then resign to a life with nothing left to do.

I prefer to wake each morning thanking God for the infinite beauty of creation, the innumerable blessings of all the people in my life, and the limitless possibilities of that day. And maybe say thanks for a few other things otherwise my morning prayer would be, you know, a list.

Dance Card

Through my several bouts of severe depression and now ALS, I have had several dances with Death, looking deeply into her eyes and clutching awkwardly for her hands. I find her gaze neither frightening nor alluring, her hold neither a repulsive vice grip nor an easy relief. No, Death's grasp is light, and she moves with quick, purposeful steps. For Death's purpose in this tryst is not to repulse, woo or claim you for herself, but merely to pass you on to your next Partner for the joy and love of the Everlasting Dance.

Sunrise

Severe depression is absolutely debilitating. Life turns inward, reducing all sense of the outside world to the equivalent of looking through a keyhole. When trapped by depression, my entire being would collapse beneath crushing thoughts of failure, unworthiness, and pain, and I was paralyzed against making decisions or dealing with even the basics of everyday life. Daytime warped into an ugly dream and nighttime a restless mist as I faced the world physically and emotionally curled up like a frightened armadillo. Even the answers to simple questions like "Are you thirsty?" became frighteningly difficult to answer and resulted in "I don't know."

My last bout was in 2000, when only intensive outpatient therapy and medication gave me the ability to peek out from the armadillo ball. The therapist gave me an assignment: go do something outside of the house every week. A group of friends from church invited me to join them on a weekly trip to minister to people at a nursing home. This was perfect, I thought. I wouldn't need to drive, and I could hide among my friends.

The nursing home was a state-run institution for people on Medicaid who had no other choices. Patient care and cleanliness were kept to a taxpayer-financed minimum. We gathered with about 20 people in the dining room, sang songs, read from the Bible, and talked. Most of the residents were obviously hungry for contact with others, sitting or standing around tables and chatting eagerly with my church friends. I neither wanted to join in a lively group conversation nor be obviously alone, so I moved to sit down next to a man who had remained along the wall by himself all evening.

He was in his 50s and as I approached, he said, "I have AIDS." In my depression, I couldn't register any implications to his words, so I sat down. He introduced himself as Bob, and I survived the first week of my assignment with a minimum of talk.

As the weeks went by, Bob and I became friends, clinging to each other in our aloneness – mine self-imposed, his pressed upon him by society. Our talks became deep, personal, and intensely real, and I opened up to him even as my life began to open out of its ball.

Then came the week Bob wasn't in the dining room. Worried, I asked an assistant where he was. She went upstairs to check in his room, then returned to say Bob wanted to see me there. I went upstairs, knocked and entered the room, his emaciation and ashen skin barely registering through my fog. There were no flowers, no letters or cards, no pictures, and no roommate in his double room. The nursing home wouldn't give a roommate to an AIDS patient. Bob was totally alone and probably had not felt a kind touch for a long time. "I'm going to my aunt's house tomorrow," he said. "She won't speak to me, but I only have a few days left and I don't want to die here. Would you baptize me before I go?" His eyes were pleading with life's last rays of hope. "Why me?" I asked. "Would you like me to get my pastor?"

"No. You have all this hurt in you, but you can still take time for me, to get to know me and talk to me about Jesus. You are the kind of person I want to baptize me." We hugged and wept until we were spent. We thanked God for making that horrific time and filthy place sacred. And God's light blazed through the deepest ebony of every dark corner of my mind, banishing forever that murky un-life of severe depression.

I learned a lesson that day that has proved invaluable to weathering the storm that is ALS. Sharing the journey and being open with others at a deep, personal level are essential for finding a balance to life. While the journey will still be difficult, bringing fellow travelers along with me on the ride will bring light to the darkness and sacredness to the profanity of a life twisted by debilitating disease.

SCALLOPS

"I slept and dreamt that life was joy. I awoke and saw that life was service. I acted and, behold, service was joy."

Tagore

Scallops are lovely shells to behold. Stunning in form, perfect in symmetry, and beautiful in color, they are attractive and desirable. Who wouldn't want that in life?

Most of us know people who are like scallops. Attractive, with beautiful homes and seemingly perfect lives, these people have built a façade, a shell that is the envy of everyone. Perhaps you even spend part of your life collecting, polishing, and displaying the beautiful scallops in your life. I used to.

But turn a scallop shell over if you have a chance. They are scratched and pitted, often with ragged edges – in other words, just like our lives. Everyone, even those whose lives seem the most perfect, has that ragged side, that "stuff," that they are forced to confront and deal with that causes stress and heartache, holding them back from becoming the people they could be. And turning a scallop shell over reveals its true character. For millennia, scallop shells have been used as bowls, cups, spoons, scoops, and shovels – used as tools for serving.

I honestly believe people are brought together more by our imperfections than by our "perfections." Most of us try and hide the imperfect parts of our lives until something dramatic happens, flipping that shell over for all to see. And, as we stand aghast at our imperfection that has just been shown to the whole world, we find others ready to hold us, comfort us, and reassure us that we are not alone. As our vulnerabilities bring us together, we see opportunities to serve each other and, through our serving, the world becomes a better place.

If only we spent less time trying to polish the shame and hurt away from the front of our lives and more time opening ourselves up for service to others. We can never make our lives perfect, but we can make the world better.

DIAGNOSIS, ACT III

From an email I sent on Thursday, April 19, 2007, 3:01 pm:

At my visit to the neurologist last month I displayed the first signs of upper motor neuron damage – when testing reflexes in my left leg, both legs jumped. It also takes me a couple of strides to get into a normal walking motion. This means that the motor control system (upper motor neurons) is confused. The net result is that all known diseases are ruled out except for ALS.

This really doesn't change much from a practical standpoint, although a diagnosis does provide access to some drug trials, and there is one in particular that seems to hold promise of extending life that I will try and enroll in later this summer or early fall. A diagnosis does give some clearer form to our expectations of "what" will happen to my body, but the "when" is still indefinable. I am still on an abnormally slow decline. Although my walking gait is different, my leg strength is pretty good and my breathing is fine as are my balance and ability to chew and swallow. I am officially into year four of a disease that kills most victims within three to five years. I continue to use alternative medicine in addition to seeing the people at the ALS clinic.

My employer's leadership is now aware of the situation and has been very supportive, providing me with a lightweight notebook, speech-recognition software, and, most importantly, a no-travel promise (in writing!).

We spoke with our children when Michelle was home for Spring break; my sense is that having a name to put on this is both fearful and somehow comforting as the unknown is given form. They understand what changes to expect to happen to me and why we need to start talking about either renovating our house or moving (and, therefore, why they need to clean and organize!). They also know that this is not genetic and does not change who they are, whose they are, or what they can do in their lives. We also reassured them that we will continue to fight the progression of this disease with all we have while continuing to live our lives normally. All this does not mean that life is not difficult for Suzanne or the children as they struggle to make sense of what life might feel like without me there as a physical presence, but every day we find examples of grace, joy, humor, and beauty that continue to give us a fullness of life.

As always, we remain more focused on how to make life count than on how to make it simply last. The lack of business travel provides opportunity for me to work on community, church, and global development/justice efforts that allow me to serve and positively impact the lives of others as well as see my family every day, all of which has importance to me well beyond that found at work. In fact, a great victory for us came on Tuesday when a school building referendum that Suzanne and I have been working on for four years passed with a substantial majority. We are also discussing whether it makes sense to have me go on disability so I may volunteer my time to other community development and education needs while I am still mobile. I don't know where this will take us, but I am excited about the possibilities. The Thursday before Easter another man in Batavia with ALS passed away. He began showing symptoms more than a year after I did, and his death is another impetus for me to search for ways I can impact others' lives.

Your prayers and support continue to be incredibly clear and valued reflections of God's grace and love. Many of you have asked how to help, and there are very many things that we do and will need help with. Please know that we will not be afraid to ask for that help, but the best thing people can continue to do for me is provide me with opportunities to serve others. Every chance I have to witness in words, song, or action is another defiant proclamation of just how little this disease can truly take from me.

VOLUNTOLD

"Come on, Michelle. Time for you to go help out at the flower sale," we tell our eldest. "But I didn't sign up for that," she protests. "Exactly. That's why we had to sign up for you." "Ugh," she says with a slight eye-roll. "Voluntold again."

We have staged this vignette in countless variations with all of our children. They are generally good sports about it, and they have learned that, no matter the protests, they will open their shells to give, serve, and gather community. When they need a little persuading, we simply remind them of what all has been done for and given to them.

JOHN AND MATTHEW VOLUNTEERING IN EL SALVADOR

Of course, we haven't just thrown them out there without any guidance. Suzanne and I teach them about how the world is in need and how their gifts can help. And we model the behaviors we expect of them, serving, giving, and gathering together. To the point of, when asked to describe our family in one word, Michelle chose 'ubiquitous'. "We're everywhere," she said. We may need to start an escrow account for their future therapy, but we will have done our best to instill in our children a sense of gratitude for all they have and the habit of giving back.

Although Suzanne is much more of a natural at this business of helping others than me – I've seen her volunteer to think of ways to volunteer – both of us had to be taught how to serve. Our own parents encouraged us and gave us examples. More than that, though, every time I read Scripture I find God signing me up to care for the sick, the poor, and the outcast. I've been voluntold to build relationships and communities that celebrate, uplift, and heal all of creation. And I have often protested, thinking I don't have the time, energy, money, or talent to make any real difference. Each time, though, God finds a way to show me the needs that exist and reminds me of all the gifts I've been given. Even in the midst of the turbulent storms of this disease, God continually shows me other people living in pain and fear and reminds me of the gifts of peace I have been given and of the wonderful, supportive communities surrounding me. I hear God saying "Look at these children of mine. They need what you have. Go. Give them a hug, a kind word, an email." Yes, God knows about the Internet.

And God doesn't simply voluntell me to do the work without providing help for the task. God gave us an example of how to make this happen. Machiavelli wrote, "If you wish to have help building a boat, do not teach your neighbors to use a hammer and chisel, rather give them a passion for the sea." God, through Scripture and the life of Jesus, gives us a beautiful vision of a world where people do justice, love mercy, and walk humbly with God. It is a picture where all are comforted, clothed, sheltered, fed, anointed, honored, loved, and at peace – with no fear of losing any of these things. This is a picture I passionately wish to help paint. Won't you join me?

HORN REBORN

From an email I sent on Tuesday, July 31, 2007, 6:23 pm:

This past Sunday our daughter Michelle and I played a horn duet at church. This sounds like such a simple statement of fact, but under that fact lays a glorious cacophony of emotions, thoughts, and memories that will buoy me up and give joy to my life for a long time. My playing wasn't perfect, but it felt like the finest offering I've ever given because it came from every part of my being.

I played on a natural horn, a horn without valves. Last Christmas, one of my sisters gave me an English translation of a 19th-century method book on how to play natural horn as well as the four Mozart concertos published for natural horn (as originally composed), and I started learning the techniques on my modern horn. I soon realized that the size, shape, and weight of a modern instrument was unsuited for the old techniques and still difficult for me to manage, so through the magic of eBay and the financial support of my family, I bought a used replica of a late-18th- century Austrian natural horn in April.

Three simple hoops. I was immediately struck by the simplicity of the natural horn design when I unpacked it from its box. Without the modern horn's valves and Gordian knot of tubing to support them, a natural horn is a lightweight single tube folded into three simple hoops. This is all I need to once again experience the beauty of playing music – the rest simply isn't necessary.

I couldn't help but reflect on how, as always, horn has provided a context and means of expression to mirror my life and feelings. Since the onset of my disease, Suzanne

MODERN HORN

and I have been ever more clearly focused on constantly asking what really matters in life, what gives life meaning and purpose. For me, the answers lie in three simple statements – do justice, love kindness, and walk humbly with our God. While my modern life certainly has its own Gordian knot of complexity and challenges, all God asks me to do in life is folded into three simple actions. I've found that this is all I need to experience the fullness and beauty of life God wants for me – the rest simply is not only unnecessary, but is distracting and sometimes even hurtful.

Just because the concept of the natural horn is simple does not make it easy to play.

After teaching myself to play any number of Renaissance instruments, trumpet, baritone, organ, several woodwinds and, to a large extent, piano, this is the hardest thing I've ever attempted musically. Playing natural horn requires more air and focus than a modern horn (already a notoriously difficult instrument) and an incredible amount of finesse and synchronization between embouchure and hand movements inside the bell. Daily practice is necessary to develop strength and consistency. Even with my high level of motivation, I am so grateful to Suzanne, who not only reminds me of my need to play but supports me in taking the time it requires – even when that time comes at the expense of other valuable activities.

As with the horn, so with God's requirements of us. Do justice, love kindness, and walk humbly with God – it looks so simple, so easy, but the reality of making it happen is so difficult. How often do I want people to get what I think they deserve, rather than what God thinks they deserve? How often do I actively work toward the goal of giving all of God's children access to the fullness of life God wants for them? Or, instead do I take the easier route – talking about others behind their backs and ignoring people's needs rather than sitting with them and learning their pains, joys, and perspectives so that I might simply meet their needs without preconditions or future ramifications? On walking humbly, it is difficult to keep God always in correct alignment in my life – as Lord, Creator, Redeemer, and Sanctifier of everything I am, know, and experience. It is easy to think my understanding of God is the right one and, if yours is different, to think yours wrong rather than seeking to learn what you know and being open to changing my ideas. And it is so incredibly easy to think I am somehow better or more important than someone else.

It takes much focus and time to get any of these things right once, much less consistently. My thoughts can wander inappropriately. (Hmmm, is it better to do the laundry or support my child/friend/spouse in their joys or needs? Or, is it really worth hurting someone in order to get what I want? Or, that person in the office drives me insane – I'm going to see if Mike feels the same way). But like playing horn, hopefully daily practice will build the strength and consistency I need to get more than glimpses of the beautiful life God wants for me. And I am so thankful for all of you who have supported me with your prayers, words, and actions. Being surrounded by so many disciples makes it easier to keep priorities straight, and you will never know how much I cherish your words back to me and how often I go back to your messages for strength when my thoughts darken. Your thoughts and prayers are clearly part of the reason for the peace and grace that have been given to me.

How Are You Today?

"How are you today?" is such a common, simple question. Unless you have ALS. There is so much physical wrongness today and even more visible on the horizon. There are indignities and humiliations to face, some of which have been going on so long they have warped any notion of normalcy. Each movement, each breath, each swallow is at once a formidable challenge for the present, a haunting echo of the past, and a sinister foreshadowing of the future. And there are concerns I don't want to admit to myself, let alone others.

How am I today? I could easily avoid the question by sulking in my room. I could wall myself off, choosing to not get involved and to minimize my exposure to other people. I could cower in fear of what I can't do today or what others might think of me.

But today I was given the grace of opening my eyes and seeing my loved ones. None of us can choose just how many of those opportunities we have left, but each of us does have a different choice. We can choose to either waste this day wallowing in self-pity, anger or fear or we can rejoice in the opportunities this day brings to love, learn, laugh, and be a positive influence on our world.

Each and every day is a gift. And it is right and good to say thanks for the gifts we are given. But saying thanks isn't enough. The greatest thanks the giver wishes is for that gift to be used to its greatest benefit and enjoyed in the greatest possible way. And so it is with this day, this masterpiece of a canvas lacking only your unique touch to be perfectly completed. The Giver of the gift of this day – a day abundant in promise, opportunity, joy, and love – desires our spoken thanks but delights in our making exuberant, extravagant use of this day for the benefit of all around us.

This is not a day to sulk in silence. This is a day to blow the horn of plenty so that everyone might hear it.

This is not a day to hoard our gifts behind a dam. This is a day to let justice roll down like a mighty water.

This is not a day to close our shells and hide in fear. This is a day to say "send me."

This is not just today. This is every day. Let's rejoice and be glad in it.

How am I today? I am fantastic – now let's get to work making this world more beautiful, joyful, and just.

Surprise

From an email I sent on Saturday, July 25, 2009, 5:55 pm:

Hi everyone!

Thank you all for being such a tremendous support group for me and my family. You are all wonderful and beautiful people!

Well, Thursday was my latest foray into the neurologist's office at the ALS clinic. This is a now a four-year relationship (begun after my previous neurologist gave me three years to live), but I have begun to dread each one of these visits more. Not that I don't like the people there – they are very kind and competent. And frankly, where else can I go to talk biochemistry with a world-renowned clinician and researcher who wears Snoopy ties? Yes, I am a geek. And, his wife was on the short list for Supreme Court nominees. It's not often you can talk with someone whose spouse had an interview in the Oval Office with the President and who had to endure the accompanying media glare.

No, it's simply recognizing where I am versus where I've been and where I am going. For example, two years ago I could walk the 2.25 miles from the train station to the office, five months ago I was wheeled into the lobby but could walk back to the exam room with help, and yesterday I had a difficult time even standing up on the scale to be weighed. From now on, I will need to be put into a lift to be weighed like vegetables in a produce scale. But given how much research we've done and how much experience we have dealing with my particular disease progression, we don't expect surprises.

Unfortunately, we got a surprise. I have lost 24 pounds in a little less than five months, likely all of it muscle mass. The cause of this is probably a combination of accelerating metabolism and me tiring out while eating, eating more slowly, and becoming full more quickly. We will begin immediately combating this by trying to push as much high-calorie, high-fat food into me as possible. This strategy, however, may not be enough, and we may have other decisions to make.

Warning – difficult material below

For those of you who don't hear us talk much, the following may be raw and uncomfortable for you. For us, it is simply real and not something to fear, hide, or sanitize. Many of you have heard me say I am grateful for the gifts that have been given to me by ALS. One of those gifts is time – as opposed, say, to someone who drops over with a pulmonary embolism. Another gift is something a friend of mine with ALS calls clarity to the journey. What she means is that to some extent people with ALS can choose how they die. We have three options: starvation; suffocation (respiratory failure due to not being physically able to breathe); or drowning (respiratory failure due to lungs filling up with fluid from pneumonia).

I, in conjunction with Suzanne and my family, will prayerfully consider whether we should aggressively combat starvation and have a feeding tube (PEG) placed into my stomach. While starvation is certainly not any immediate concern, I probably have a six- to nine-month window to make this decision before my breathing is too weak to risk surgery. A PEG does not necessarily replace normal chewing and swallowing, but provides a means to supplement nutritional intake by pushing food from something that looks like a Spritz cookie dough press through a plastic tube with a valve (think air mattress inflation valve) that goes directly into my stomach. Or, for the younger (or younger-at-heart) crowd, imagine a beer bong directly into the stomach. I guess one potential benefit could be the reduction to our beer budget if I simply ram cheap swill in. Or not.

We certainly invite your prayers, suggestions, comments, and input to this decision-making process. I do, however, request your understanding that, in the end, this is a private decision we ask that you honor. We will continue to need your caring support no matter what we decide.

End of difficult material

Here is my functional ratings scale chart:

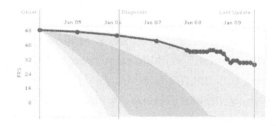

Although this is virtually unchanged for the last eight months, the graph is a little deceiving right now. I expect some major point reductions in the next few months as we will probably start bi-pap about two to four hours per evening for breathing assistance – my breathing capacity is now at 69% (exactly where I expected it would be) – and I am unsure how much longer I can feed myself at all or walk even with assistance. However, even these point reductions would not take me down to the 90th percentile line I was on before starting Lithium. I remain convinced Lithium is helping me. I'm also pursuing a liver bile acid that has been tested in Huntington's disease, Alzheimer's, and ALS (but funding ran out for the ALS research before it was completed – the story of our lives). The hope for this chemical is that it would keep cells from committing suicide at such a high rate, although finding a source for it has been problematic. We are also still fighting insurance for coverage of the diaphragm pacing system that would exercise my diaphragm muscles electronically and keep them stronger longer.

Some real joys for me lately have been an Amazon Kindle for reading and a used electric scooter (donated by a friend from church) for getting around with some independence. Both of these were fantastically useful to me on our recent short vacation to Door County (we had a lift put on the back of the van to transport the scooter). It was liberating for me to be able to take myself the three quarters of a mile from hotel to beach, read a book and, after finishing it, buy a new one right from the beach. And it felt good to free the rest of my family to do the things they wanted to do. We have also created a new front sidewalk forming a second ramp into our house. This was important to me for safety reasons. Previously, if I was to be seated in the front of the house and we had a kitchen fire, there would have been no way for me to get out.

We also were thrilled to have family and many friends at our church on July 5 for a vow renewal ceremony commemorating our 25th wedding anniversary. We had a great time planning it, and everything went very well. We had a full Eucharistic service, wrote new vows, decorated the altar with perennials which we used to plant an anniversary garden outside our bedroom window, and shared cake, coffee, and punch afterwards. This wonderful day was simply an obvious reminder of how there is love, grace, and joy in every day. My hope for all of you is that you would feel this as keenly as I do. Life truly is beautiful.

No Holding Back

(Written as a gift to Suzanne on our 25th anniversary)

My dearest friend,
our hugs are but glimpses of the closeness of our beings,
yet soaring views.

Harbors for shelter and solace, recharging and revelry, they melt distance away.

What will we do
when you longingly reach for respite and
piningly find
no holding back?

My loving wife,
entwined hands and arms are our tender,
defiant claims we are
never alone.

Rocks of vulnerability, publicly intimate, they
bare
togetherness.

What will we do
when you desperately clutch for strength and
achingly feel
no holding back?

My beloved,
Together we've learned time is elusive, fears are
fruitless and
only love matters.

Love makes moments eternity, refines blemish
and reveals
the face of God.

And so I will
love you fully, extravagantly and urgently, with
no holding back.

Man's Best Friend?

I love dogs. Actually, I love all animals, especially dogs. Big dogs – my favorite was a neighbor's Irish Wolfhound that I cared for a while in college.

When Suzanne and I were married, the combination of her allergies and our small apartment kept my wish for a large dog on hold. We did, with some reluctance on my part, get a toy poodle. Hardly a man's dog, I thought. At least we never gave the poodle a fancy haircut.

Predictably, my love for animals overcame my bias and the poodle, Scamper, became "my" dog. As did Hollibelle, our second small poodle. Hollibelle never lets me out of her sight.

In spring 2008, I had Hollibelle out in the front yard. Over the past year, I had fallen a dozen times and had at least two concussions, but I still refused to use the electric scooter in the garage that a friend had loaned me. Stubbornness is another ALS symptom. Since I always land on my head when I fall, a friend told me to keep leading with my head – I never seem to sustain much damage.

As I was walking Hollibelle, a neighbor rounded the corner with her dog. Hollibelle took off toward the other dog, anxious to say hello. I panicked at the sight of our retractable leash unwinding like a fishing line with a great white shark on the hook. I braced for the tug when the leash ran out, grabbing it with both hands because I knew my grip was too weak.

I used to think walking a 10-pound poodle was about the most unmanly circumstance in my life. I was wrong. Having my face planted in the garden mulch after being pulled over by a 10- pound poodle is.

And so it came to pass that I decided to use the electric scooter and, later, a full-featured power wheelchair. But my dog trouble isn't over yet. Hollibelle and daughter Michelle's five-pound Yorkshire terrier love to dance and play right in front of my chair as I drive around the house, limiting me to moving about six inches at a time lest I run one of the tiny beasts over.

Wheelchair Shopping

From an email I sent on Saturday, Oct. 3, 2009, 10:25 pm:

Does anyone remember a time when buying a car involved selecting from a huge features list where, if you wanted one thing, you needed to buy two others? Believe me, Detroit never had anything on wheelchair manufacturers.

Although I'll get whatever my medical team recommends and insurance will pay for, vehicle shopping is hard-wired into the Y chromosome so I went Windows-shopping. I found a chair I think will satisfy my needs – comfort for 18 hour/day use, a 16-20 mile range and good drivability indoors and out – and downloaded the price list for grins. The price list is 12 pages long.

It started so innocently with a base price of $10,156, with five standard color choices. Other than wondering what the point of the spurious $6 was, I was feeling pretty happy with my choice and thought I'd check out a few options.

The first option section is seating. That's right, the base price of a power wheelchair doesn't include anywhere to, you know, sit. A chair with power tilt, recline, and up/down functions (to prevent sores and ease transfers) costs another $16,665. As you would expect for such a low, low price, you also need to select a mesh or leatherette cover for $586-$899 or you're sitting directly on foam. Does leatherette come from cowette?

Then comes power. The base motor is OK for indoors, but makes you more vulnerable than a 3-legged blind opossum when crossing the street. Enough speed for residential areas is

$1877 more, and if you need to cross four-lane streets before the little red man lights up, pop $2742 for the high-performance rig.

And on it goes. If you want the machine to be something other than foyer art, you'd better order the $982 battery pack. Want to steer? Select one of six joysticks, ranging up to $1442. Stop there and you get the joystick in a box – to have it actually mounted on the chair costs $897 extra.

The cost for a fully-loaded powerchair tricked out with headlights, horn, backpack storage, padding, leg raisers/extenders, and an extra joystick for a caregiver (when I can no longer work one myself) can top $48,000.

Price point now established, I continued shopping for electric transport.

I found the Model S by Tesla Motors. It is all electric, features Lithium-ion batteries that recharge in 45 minutes, and seats five plus two fold-down child seats – seven seats in three rows. It does –zero to 60 in 5.6 seconds, has a 120 mph top speed, and has a 300 mile range before charging.

In spite of a recent Washington Post article showing Medicare pays power chair dealers at 2.5 times their cost, I would never suggest power chair manufacturers (all three of them) would take advantage of disabled people or Medicare reimbursement guidelines. But the Model S does look a bit more substantial, and it comes standard with climate control as well as entertainment and navigation systems – all of which would be nice on a power chair as would be automobile-like financing options. And the Model S has two power tilt/recline/up/down seats with all interior surfaces covered in real leather – no extra charge. Give the Model S a joystick control and I'll make do with my loaner chair indoors and spend my days bombing around the countryside in serious style.

FRIDAY WITH BEETHOVEN

A summer Friday night was one of those rare, sweet treats in life that simply must be shared. After I had had a week of sulking, Suzanne dropped Matthew and me (in my power chair) at the train station. Once on board one of our wonderfully accessible commuter trains, the two of us enjoyed great conversation and laughter on the way downtown. Upon arrival, we fought our way upstream against the tide of commuter pedestrian traffic to Millennium Park. I am learning that pedestrians don't watch out for people in wheelchairs, and they seem to always congregate in front of and walk down the curb cut ramps that I need to go up and down between the street and sidewalk. I am considering some James Bond-style accessories for the wheelchair. Does "Q" make house calls?

Back to Millennium Park, where about 10,000 people had congregated to hear a free concert on a beautiful evening. And not just any concert, but my favorite piece of music, Beethoven's incomparable Ninth Symphony, the one with the "Ode to Joy" chorus at the end. Don't get me wrong, I love Bach and Mozart, too, but in my opinion they perfected composition under the rules of their day. Beethoven, particularly in the Ninth Symphony, swept all of those rules into a neat little pile and lovingly blew them up. There is even a funeral march in the first movement signifying the burial of music composition as people then knew it. Three times, at the beginning of the fourth movement, he teases us with snippets to make us think he might sell out and go back to a traditional style. Each time, Beethoven quickly says "I'm not going back there" and proceeds to conclude the symphony even more radically than he began it. My kind of guy!

Beethoven was deaf when he composed this incredibly beautiful and transformational piece of music. It is easy for us to listen to Beethoven's Ninth Symphony with our 21st-century ears and values and say "that was lovely." But doing this trivializes the reality that you have just heard the echo of a massive tectonic shift in Western history.

Art was liberated from rules and form and from the control of royalty and instead gifted to the people. Without this momentous work, first performed in a subscription concert for the general public, the grand gift of symphonic composition may have collapsed along with the ruling families of Europe. Instead, never more would a symphony be written for or debuted in a royal court. Art became of, by, and for the people, and Beethoven became the Thomas Jefferson of culture, the Ninth Symphony the declaration of independence for the arts.

Even the ideas of what constituted civil society in an age of commoners freed from royal rule took form as the Ninth's popularity gave rise to the ideal of the "gebildete", or cultured, person. One can argue that, without the Ninth, the environment of creative freedom that gave us Mahler, Strauss, Stravinsky, van Gogh, Picasso, Rodin, and Martha Graham would not have existed. One can also argue that the cultured society necessary to appreciate their art and make them popular would not have existed.

And the Ninth's themes of unity, hope, and freedom from tyranny keep it relevant today. Protesters in Tiananmen Square played recordings of it. Leonard Bernstein led a performance of it at the Brandenburg gate to celebrate the unification of Berlin, and many commemorations of the 9/11 tragedy have featured it.

Not bad for less than 75 minutes of sound penned by a man who couldn't hear. And maybe that's Beethoven's ultimate revolution – shattering the illusion of personal limitations based on external perceptions in favor of a world of infinite possibility because of who we are on the inside.

People disagree on whether Beethoven was able to compose the Ninth Symphony in spite of or because of his deafness. He often spoke about music being the voice of God. Perhaps the lack of outside distraction allowed him to focus in on what God was saying without needing to force the conversation into man-made conventions. I know from my own experience that the urgency of disability can produce a sense of boldness to do things previously outside of your comfort zone.

All of this causes me to wonder what kind of people we would be and what we might accomplish if we were able to cut out the day's distractions for a while, hear God's voice, and urgently and boldly act on what we've heard. Without caring if we are conforming to society. Maybe we would be more beautiful, radical and transformational than the world ever thought we could be, than we ever believed we could be.

BETWEEN ME AND MY DOCTOR

From an email I sent on Tuesday, Aug. 4, 2009, 11:12 pm:

My pulmonologist recommends I have a diaphragmatic pacing system implanted to assist my breathing by keeping my diaphragm muscle stronger than I am able to without the technology. The benefits of this, proven in more than 100 ALS patients, are increased energy and postponement of the decision to use a ventilator by an average of two years.

Non-ALS people who suffer spinal cord injuries are normally encouraged to opt for a diaphragmatic pacing system rather than a ventilator. It's more portable, less invasive than surgeons poking a hole in your throat and shoving an air hose in the hole, and it allows for more normal speech function. Ventilators require periodic (including every two to three hours through the night) suctioning to keep them clear of mucus and clinic visits are necessary every four to six months to have vital parts replaced; diaphragmatic pacing requires no such burdens. Many states require 24/7 in-home trained care for people on ventilators, effectively eliminating this care option for all but the wealthy; there is no special nursing care required for the diaphragmatic pacer. Plus, it's cheaper than a ventilator.

The powers-that-be at my insurance company are declining to cover the diaphragmatic pacing system costs. Their reasoning is quite clear, and it has nothing to do with my doctors' wishes or medical evidence. They are basing their decision on the likelihood that I will no longer be working at the time I need a ventilator, kicking costs down the road when I will be covered by Medicare instead of private insurance. At that time, surgery for diaphragmatic pacing will not be an option and I will need to decide whether to die by suffocation or have most of my ventilation costs paid by the taxpayers. Between me and my doctor stand corporate profits.

HONORING THE CAREGIVERS WE LOVE

In very many ways, this disease is more difficult for the spouse caregiver than the patient. And not only because of the physical, time-consuming and unpleasant caregiver tasks Suzanne (and all of my family) courageously faces each day. And not even because of the emotional trauma of watching your spouse degenerate from an active, healthy adult to the functional equivalent of a 12-month-old, shattering the dreams we once shared of this time in our lives.

We battle every day to not be defined by ALS, but we lose ground to that battle every time Suzanne is described as simply a caregiver or is used during conversation only as a conduit of information about me or when people neglect to learn about and understand her life outside of this disease. I have seen Suzanne get hurt many times, by many different people, when they refuse to acknowledge or see her as anything but my caregiver. When people talk to Suzanne, they only ask about me. When people ask what she is doing, they are only interested in what she is doing for me. People celebrate when I do something to defy this disease, but ignore Suzanne's accomplishments outside her caregiver role. In short, the world tries very hard to rob her of her individual dignity and to ignominiously confine her life within an "ALS caregiver" box.

She is so much more than that, and it saddens and angers me when people contribute to boxing her in rather than celebrating the whole person she is. Feelings of insignificance, invisibility, dehumanization, and worthlessness outside of the disease are echoed by caregivers in many different situations, and I get angry every time I see Suzanne silently tear up at an insensitive comment. She has many different gifts, interests, and accomplishments that are too often overlooked or minimized as people look past her to me. And as they are overlooked, her humanity dwindles.

We are all fighting ALS, and it has won whenever we define someone solely in terms of their relationship to the disease. I ask all those who know people upon whom the role of caregiver has been forced to uplift, dignify, and celebrate all aspects of their lives, especially those parts that demonstrate they will not let this disease claim them as well.

CONCHES

*We were born to unite with our fellows,
and to join in community with the human race.*

Cicero

Conch shells are the castle keeps of the deep – massive, spiny fortresses meant to preserve and protect their owners' solitude. I used to be like this – painfully shy, doing anything to keep people away from who I really am, avoiding crowds and social settings whenever possible, and clinging to Suzanne when avoiding others wasn't an option. I once spent five hours circling Switzerland on trains looking for a way to neighboring Austria, finally sleeping the balance of the night in a parking garage elevator, just so I wouldn't have to approach someone for help. Music was perfect for me; I could wall myself off in a practice room for hours.

But a conch can have a different purpose than protecting its resident. These shells have been blown like a horn by island people for centuries, sounding the call to bring community together to worship, share wisdom, celebrate, heal, defend against danger, and gather and share food. It has taken me a long time to understand that the idea that I can (or should) make it through life on my own is a total myth. I have always loved how I feel when helping others; how *dare* I deprive others of that feeling by burying my needs under some self-absorbed vanity that says "I can handle anything myself!"

We are social creatures, created to be our best when in relationship with others. Together we learn, do, and grow more. Together we recognize and solve more of the world's problems. Together we heal the bodies and spirits of those around us, strengthening the whole. So be bold – blow that conch you've been hiding in and be amazed by what your gathered community can do. Together.

STORYTELLING

A Prologue

Humankind has for millennia embraced the sharing of stories. Oral tradition plays a central role in defining who we are, where we have been, and our hopes for the future. The wisdom of the ages has passed down our cultural identities, faiths, ideals, and moral codes. Much of who we believe ourselves to be has been determined by countless generations of families, communities, and tribes gathering together to share stories.

Perhaps that is one reason I love the arts so much. Don't get me wrong, I love my sports, too, but the arts gather community together to share stories, images, and sound in a shared experience where there are no winners or losers. All are welcome, and your unique experience is something no one can take from you.

The beautiful paradox of our unique experiences is that, as we share them, we find that parts of them resonate and interlock with the unique experiences of others and become communal. The story that was mine becomes ours, building us up as individuals as we are validated and connecting us more tightly to each other. I am a witness to the power of storytelling as sharing my journey openly has empowered me, given me control over the narrative of my story, and brought me into closer bonds with so many people.

There are those who struggle with disease and misfortune who try to hide their stories. Whether their reasoning comes from not wanting to burden others, not wanting to make themselves vulnerable, fearing shame or contempt, or hiding the truth from themselves, I have too often seen this inwardness fester and rot people away. It is horrible to see this rot in a human being, a child of God, especially when that rot is expressed as bitterness and self-contempt. As Ludwig van Beethoven wrote in his diary, "All misfortune is mysterious and greatest when viewed alone; discussed with others it seems more endurable because one becomes entirely familiar with the things one dreads, and feels as if one has overcome it."

The telling of stories is under siege in our current culture. Technology and social media keep us connected but not gathered. We share our lives and our thoughts in trite status updates and 140-character snippets, interacting in isolation. These interactions focus much on the "I" while pushing the "we" aside. In doing so, I am concerned that we are allowing the sinews that bind us together to become brittle and easily broken. Witness what passes for political discourse lately. We must find ways to use technology to introduce us and invite us into face-to-face gathering so that our shared wisdom can once more provide the story of us.

Thank you for coming into my story, a story where ALS has no power, where God's gifts of love and beauty are always present, and where life always has purpose through giving, serving, and building community.

Please take the time to share your story widely. If you wish, to share conversation with me and others at www.steveheronemus.com or www.facebook.com/shellsbook.

Why Do We Sing?

"Life fades and withers behind us, but of our immortal and sacred soul all that remains is music."

Jean Paul Richter

"Why do we sing?" was the title of the sermon given at the Confirmation service of one of our nieces. It was a beautiful service, filled with joy as about 30 teens stood up to publicly lay claim to their faith. The sermon was great, too, focused on how the gift of music can transport us to a place and time, fill us with happiness, and lift our spirits. In the days that followed, I thought a little more about that sermon theme. I couldn't help but feel there was more to be said about the role music, and art in general, plays in our lives and how music is of God.

I believe that we are created in the image of God. To me, that doesn't mean we look like God, but that we imperfectly share some of the same qualities as God. First, God is creative. Merely contemplating the near-infinite variety of life and matter on this planet inspires shouts of the creative nature of God, and my imagination staggers if I try to extend that to what might exist throughout the vastness of the universe. The universe is beautiful and terrifying, harmonious, discordant, and awe-inspiring. Making music is similarly near-infinite in its creativity. Even if one simply hums a tune, that person's own interpretation, emotion, and soul become a part of the melody, eternally embedded in that unique creation. Music can also be both beautiful and terrifying, evoking awe in the listener. J. R. R. Tolkien, in The Silmarillion (his history of Middle Earth that precedes the Lord of the Rings trilogy), portrays creation being born of a song sung by the creator with the first-born of that creation joining in and adding their own creativity to the song. Evil comes into Middle Earth when one of the first-born tries to bend the song to his own will. I must admit that I rather like this vision, and I wouldn't be at all surprised to find that the voice of God is music.

God also heals. Whether through miracles, the God-given talents of medical care, or peace to a sorrowful heart, God offers renewal of body and spirit within this broken world. Similarly, we often comfort ourselves with music, using its restorative power to heal our hearts in times of difficulty and allowing our bodies to heal more quickly.

Most of all, music brings us together into community. Whether talking about your favorite song, singing along with your best friends to the car radio, or attending a live concert, music gathers us into a shared experience. And we do this not out of some sense of duty or competitive instinct. We do this for the sheer joy and beauty of it. God desires creation to be in harmonious relationship and built us to want and need connection with others. God promises us a more full and abundant life if we walk through it together, accompanying each other in pain and sorrow, joy and celebration. Music is a wonderful tool to help make God's promise real.

Creating, healing, bringing together. Enjoying music, or any art, is a sacred act that lifts us out of the mundane, selfish world and firmly connects us with our own spirit, our neighbors, and our Creator. Music is a blessing, a precious gift, a celebration of our image being of God. And that, I believe, is why we sing.

STUPID HUMAN TRICKS

One odd side effect of ALS is hyperreflexivity or overly sensitive reflexes. No one knows why this happens. While this can be annoying during some tasks like brushing teeth (heightened gag reflex), our daughter Claire has found a way to make the best of it.

She helps me put one knee over the other and places a dog toy on top of the foot lifted off the floor. Then, with a slight tap of my thigh, she unleashes my reflexes to send the toy hurtling across the room for the dogs to fetch. A medieval catapult has nothing over my left leg. I may not be able to walk or move my arms, but boy howdy can I play fetch!

25TH ANNIVERSARY VOWS

My Dearest Love, today I give thanks to God for binding us together and, in gratitude and love, I rededicate myself to you, rejoicing in the 25 years of marriage we've already shared.

I will share your days, wipe away the tears and laugh through the joys. I will be strength for your weakness, light in your darkness. Your dreams will be my dreams. I will inspire your hope and calm your fears. I will forgive you as we have been forgiven, accepting all that you are in unconditional and abiding love.

At your side, I promise to grow deeper in faith and stronger in our commitment to show kindness, mercy, and justice to others.

With Christ as my guide, I will love with all that I am.

WHEELCHAIR SHOPPING, PART TWO

From an email I sent on Wednesday, Nov. 18, 2009, 12:43 am:

The epic continues – at a pace only a soap opera fan could stomach.

We had a home evaluation two weeks ago to determine if our home posed any limitations on our selection of power chair. I had a sizing and medical needs evaluation on the 16th, and now my medical team and I will settle on a set of features we think I need and send that to the insurance company for approval. After the inevitable negotiations with the insurance company, we will have to decide which non-covered features we can afford to pay for ourselves and then order the chair.

Since each chair is semi-custom, delivery could take several months from the time of order. I don't anticipate getting a new chair until sometime around March - May.

Chairs that insurance will normally cover go about four miles an hour, mid-level performance is six-and-a-half mph, and high performance is eight to nine mph. For the record, speed is a safety feature in a busy environment that includes taxis and six-lane streets. There is one superchair where, at the touch of a button, the frame extends 12 inches to lengthen the wheelbase and the seat drops down for greater stability, effectively creating a 20 mph electric go-kart. Unfortunately, its big turning radius makes it suitable for outdoor use only.

Here is the really goofy thing – I added up the price for the Permobil C300 "standard" ALS power chair with all the features I know insurance will cover (no seat elevator, no "standing" position, no lights) and the list price came to nearly $30,000. There is another chair manufacturer offering a nine mph product that, with all those extra features, costs about the same. But insurance won't pay for it. The coverage position from my insurer clearly states that they will provide reimbursement for the features necessary for in-home safety, but will not reimburse for features necessary for independent living. Welcome to the Stone Age of health care.

We are seriously looking at the Permobil C500 VS.

The standing option is really a medical issue, not a convenience. Humans are created to be upright – breathing is easier and deeper (just ask any musician); respiratory illnesses are more rare; digestion works better; pressure sores, muscle stiffness and foot swelling are reduced; and bone density is maintained. For everyday living, a "stander" chair puts light switches,  elevator buttons, sinks, and refrigerator water dispensers within reach and eliminates neck strain from trying to have a conversation with standing adults. Plus it is far easier to transfer someone out of the chair when they are already standing, reducing caregiver injuries.

Our next steps are to have the power chair representative bring a Permobil C500 VS to our house to confirm that its size and maneuverability work in our home. If not, we'll go with the C300; if so, we order the "stander" and gird ourselves for battle with the insurance company. Again. In either case, this will be the most expensive vehicle I've ever owned. And I'll have to buy an aftermarket cupholder.

Addendum: I was able to get the "standing" powerchair I wanted. It has been fabulous for use at work and for conversing with others at eye level, but the best possible use came at Michelle's wedding.

Happy New Year!

From an email I sent on Friday, Jan. 8, 2010, 5:59 pm:

This is the season to take stock of what things make us happy in life. For me, this revolves around faith, family, health (yes, health, I was originally not given a chance to see this year, so every day is a good day), and friends. Many of us also make resolutions of things to do to improve ourselves, whether that be quitting smoking, spending more time with the children, losing weight, or catching up on our reading.

But should these things, however noble and worthy, be our main responses to the happiness we feel in this time of new beginnings? As I thought about this, my mind wandered, naturally, to Beethoven. Late in his life, Beethoven was not only deaf and unable to hear the masterworks he created or to indulge his love of music in any normal way, he was often sickly and bed-ridden. About two years before his death, Beethoven went through a very severe and lengthy illness that caused him to think he might very well die. Upon his recovery, he expressed his gratitude in the best way he knew how – he immediately began composing. Never mind that he would never hear it, and never mind that the slow movement for a string quartet he now composed didn't really fit as part of the larger work he had started earlier. He was simply compelled to write this music. In an unusual move, Beethoven even gave this individual movement its own title – "Holy Hymn of Thanks from a Convalescent to the Deity."

This "Holy Hymn of Thanks" is not the fiery, tempestuous Beethoven many people know. This work is Beethoven on his knees with eyes and hands lifted to heaven. He is peaceful, serene, and transcendent, caressing each note and reveling in his re-found opportunity to exercise his gift for writing music. In fact, he becomes so enraptured with giving thanks that he simply cannot contain his joy – twice in this supposedly slow movement Beethoven's music breaks out into dance.

Dance! From a man who has repeatedly been deathly ill and can't hear his own music? From a man who never found love and was abused and shunned by family? Yet Beethoven felt deeply that music was the voice of God and that it was God's gift to him to have that voice flow through him to make the world a better place. He knew of no more joyful thing than to use the gift God had given him.

So I will resolve this year to be profoundly thankful for the gifts I've been given and to use those gifts to make the world around me a better place. Then a happy new year won't depend on what I want, but will flow from what God has given me. And since Beethoven can dance without hearing, I will joyfully and thankfully dance without standing.

ROBODAD RELEASE 1.0

With my PEG feeding tube and diaphragm pacing system, I have five wires and a two-foot long section of clear vinyl garden hose (sort of) sticking out of my abdomen. The wires enable me to plug into an alternate reality of better breathing while the hose is for stupid party tricks – "I wonder what will happen if we shoot Everclear and puréed habaneros directly in his stomach." Or "Let's see what kind of reaction we get if we snake the free end out of my fly."

I guess the wires have potential, too. "If we switch the polarity, can he double as a vacuum cleaner?" At least I'd get some chores done around the house. Extra credit for anyone who caught the Matrix reference – I'm still a big geek, um, fan. Combine this package with a wheelchair that can take me from lying down to fully upright and some makeup, and we have the beginnings of a really cool Halloween display. Who wants to play Igor?

Entourage

I cry in agony as the lab technicians try to move me into various positions to get a series of CT scans. My abdomen is on fire, I am exhausted from lack of sleep and weak from too little food both before my surgery three days earlier and since. Even under normal circumstances I don't breathe well while lying on my back, and the pain has made my breathing even more shallow. Of course, on my back is exactly where the technicians need me to be. Between the pain and the inability to breathe, the room faded in and out of focus as I fought to remain conscious. In this scene, it would be so easy to feel utterly alone.

I try to try and separate my mind from the pain I begin to rewind history to figure out how, exactly, I wound up at the emergency room of our local hospital, me in the radiology lab with Suzanne waiting for me in the examination room. We had traveled from the Chicago area to Atlanta to have a diaphragm pacing system implanted to exercise my diaphragm to keep it strong and help inflate my lungs. This is not new technology, having been developed for people with spinal cord injuries and in use for these people for more than five years without any adverse experiences. Its application in people with ALS, however, was not yet approved by the FDA even though a clinical study with 80+ patients had been complete for more than a year. Because of this, only one doctor in the country was allowed to do the surgery right when I needed it. And, it is standard procedure to place a feeding tube at the same time the DPS is being implanted.

I had been caught in an odd window of time. My personal research led me to believe the diaphragm pacer was a great idea, and the surgery had to be done before my respiratory and diaphragm function declined much further than it was. There was no telling how long the FDA would take in deciding to approve or deny the use of the device in people with ALS, so we and my pulmonologist searched for someone to do the procedure "off-label". We thought a doctor at Northwestern might do it and we scheduled a time. The Friday before Monday's surgery Suzanne got the call that our surgeon would not be allowed to do the "off-label" procedure so an urgent hunt for a new surgeon and hospital began. The surgical team at Northwestern was kind enough to track down colleagues in Atlanta who were experienced in the techniques and willing to take us on.

Of course, another drawback to having surgery without FDA approval meant my insurance would not cover the costs. They had no problems paying for it in spinal cord injury cases, but even though it is the exact same procedure and my doctors and I had petitioned them incessantly, the powers-that-be at the insurance company would not budge on their policy. The quaint notion that you and your doctor control your medical decisions is a cruel farce. Insurance bureaucrats do. I joked with the insurance case worker that I should go horseback riding and get thrown until I broke my spine. I mean, the end result of paralysis is the same, I would just get there more quickly. "Would you cover it then?" I asked. "Of course." she replied. So much for their motto "Your health is number one." It should be more like "We cover number one." That's both effectively ambiguous and truthful.

While on the subject of insurance companies, does it strike anyone else as odd that this is the only industry that profits by NOT providing the services it sells? I have been a consultant to a number of insurance companies, and they were all apparently given a license to print cash. As the industry saying goes, "there are no bad risks, only bad premiums."

Suzanne and I decided to drive to Atlanta as we felt there were so many unknowns in how I would do navigating airports and on the flight itself. Who knew how the TSA would react to someone with 20 feet of electrical wire coiled inside him? We arranged to have our at-home children stay with friends while we were gone, contacted family and friends, and made an advanced directives document. We were told this surgery should be routine and low risk, but administering any kind of general anesthetic to a person with a compromised respiratory system can be problematic.

Our trip down featured a two-hour delay; I-65 was closed due to trucks overturned during a tornado – in January. The ride home came in the aftermath of a terrible mid-Atlantic winter storm and the roads rutted with packed snow and ice bounced our minivan mercilessly, twisting the knife in my side that was my feeding tube. Suzanne called my doctor when we were a few hours from home, and he suggested we go straight to the emergency room. I just wanted to go home, but Suzanne insisted on the ER.

I was admitted as an inpatient after the ER staff found a massive infection and hematoma. I was discharged after treatment over four days with massive antibiotic doses, only to go back to the hospital a week later when the pain was back and my feeding tube had failed completely. A wonderful gastroenterologist, who happened to be on call in the ER, immediately diagnosed the problem; the inner backing of my tube had pulled out of my stomach and into the abdominal cavity. A PEG feeding tube is like a huge pierced earring with a hollow post. There is a bumper inside the stomach that is like the backing of an earring, holding the post from sliding out. With my backing out of my stomach, everything that went down the tube accumulated in the abdominal cavity and became infected. He operated immediately to place a new tube. I stopped breathing on the table but was fortunately revived without resorting to a tracheostomy.

A long, lonely road? Not even close. My surgery was funded through a recital given by a dear friend, attended by more than one hundred members of our community. Before we left, our pastor held a prayer service for me, attended by people from all walks of life. Even children took time to put their hands on me and pray. A group of women knitted and prayed over a shawl for me. I was covered with that shawl up to the very moment I was wheeled into surgery, and it has stayed with me through all my hospitalizations. An uncle took off from work to drive Suzanne and me to Atlanta and to help with my care on the trip, and my parents flew from Arizona to Atlanta to be with us. A childhood friend, our pastor's wife, and my boss visited me in the Atlanta hospital, and I had numerous visitors in our local hospital. And Suzanne, ever my partner, friend, and advocate never left my side. My physical condition may have been frail, but I felt the strength of untold hundreds lifting me, carrying me at every step. This whole process was never about me, it was about us.

Power Wheelchair Wish List

Here's an homage to the vehicle option list, lovingly crafted after years of user experience.

Powertrain

Boy racer package	More horsepower. Lots more. I once was pulled over by the police for speeding on

	my bicycle. It would be a proud day for me if I were stopped for speeding in my chair. If someone thinks they can engineer an indoor / outdoor hybrid drive using my 300hp Jaguar motor, call me.
Adaptive suspension	Something that can go from asphalt to sidewalk to lawn without needing to check if my dental insurance is paid.

Safety

Armrest-mounted Taser	I know of three people with ALS who were robbed while out in their powerchairs. Dante needs to describe a new circle of hell to house the robbers.
Fuzzy padded handcuffs	Get your mind out of the gutter. These are to keep my hands on the controls while

	bouncing over rough terrain. I'll take mine in tiger stripes.
Truck horn	The base horn sounds like a squeak toy, and I've nearly gotten run over twice.
Emergency beacon	In case I accidentally drive off a cliff. Don't put it past me.

Convenience

Retractable umbrella	For sun and rain.
GPS	No, not a navigator for me – I know where I'm going. A locater for Suzanne for when I wander off for hours.
Seat heater	The chair is made in Sweden. You'd think they would have thought of this already.
Cupholder	Really, how hard could this be?

Entertainment

iPod dock	Control iPod with power chair joystick.
Mini keg cooler	With height-adjustable "krazy" straw. There's no law against driving a powerchair under the influence.
Fuzzy padded handcuffs	Oops. Covered these already.

Accessories

Sidecar	So I can take my sweetheart or granddaughter out in style.
Lawn mower deck	To tow behind me. I went into a hardware store and asked for this. The poor, eager-to-please salesman took me seriously and started looking in a catalog. After a couple minutes, I didn't have the heart to continue the charade.

Snow plow	Just trying to be useful.
Flame-thrower	To clear inattentive pedestrians from my path. There's nothing quite like being stuck in the middle of Chicago's Michigan Avenue as the light changes because some idiots won't let me get up the sidewalk ramp.

COLD WEATHER, COLD FACTS

Winter's cold and snow are no big deal for those of us born and raised in the Midwest. We shrug them off as either something to endure with an affect of invincibility or as opportunities for fun which Southerners will never understand. By opportunities for fun I mean acts of idiocy, like joining the Polar Bear Club by swimming in Lake Michigan on New Year's Day when the 33-degree water is far warmer than the air.

My approach to winter used to incorporate both strategies. I slipped into flip-flops to take the dog out no matter how deep the snow and scorned hats except when a fashion statement was in order. I had a great hill for tobogganing at the end of my street. The fact that the hill was in a deep forest didn't bother me until I hit a tree and ruined my knees The next time I tobogganed I made sure to pile snow up by that tree; of course I hit a different one, but the extra risk just made for more fun.

Another fun Wisconsin winter adventure is ice fishing for sturgeon in Lake Winnebago. Wisconsin law makes this more fun by outlawing normal fishing with line, hook, and bait in favor of spears. So this activity involves sitting on a block of ice, staring down a hole in the ice, waiting for one of the massive, 150-pound, fish to happen by. One of the massive, *inedible* fish. I tried this once and, at the risk of revealing some centuries-old male secret, I surmise the only possible reason people do this is to drink much brandy away from the women-folk.

I donned my cloak of invincibility every winter, even after my diagnosis. At every clinic visit to the Lois Insolia ALS Center at Northwestern, my doctors would ask if I wanted a flu shot, and I would decline every time. I never had the flu, why would I need a vaccine? My pulmonologist would also ask if I wanted to start her recommended regimen of respiratory therapies. This regimen consists of a device that pounds the chest with dozens of bursts of air per second to loosen secretions, a nebulizer to deliver medicine that opens the airways, a machine to force coughs to move the secretions out of the lungs, and a suction machine to get the gunk out of the mouth. Whew, it makes me tired just describing it. The principal idea behind all this is to reduce the risk of pneumonia since a person with ALS doesn't breathe deeply enough to dry out the bottom of the lungs or cough hard enough to clear the lungs of mucus. Needless to say, I refused these as well.

I refused to do these things because I was fine. The disease was progressing slowly in me, and I never got sick. Except for this little ALS thing I've never been healthier. I wasn't one of *those* patients that needed all that stuff. I was invincible.

2011 was a busy year for me. Between work, serving on the church council and the board of our high school's theatre boosters and mentoring a small group of high school students, we were preparing for Michelle's wedding, looking forward to Claire's high school graduation and college acceptance letters, and to participating in the festivities surrounding the inaugural year of our city's new performing arts centre that I had spent four years shepherding into existence. I was out and in crowds often.

The sniffles started a week before Christmas, and a cough developed a couple of days later. Suzanne called our clinic, and the staff thought I should be checked there on Dec. 23, but I didn't want that. It was too close to Christmas and I didn't want to ruin the holiday. Besides, I was still invincible. And fine.

Soon I couldn't lie down because I would cough up fluid, but I couldn't cough it up far enough so I would choke. Suzanne called the EMTs twice; they put a tube down my nose to suction out as much as they could. We attended church on Christmas Eve, but I had to leave early because of coughing and choking. We did get home to watch our kids open one gift each, our tradition, Suzanne had to call 9-1-1 again at about 1:00 am because I couldn't breathe. We went to the emergency room at our local hospital where they tried for hours to calm the cough and suction out whatever they could. We welcomed Christmas morning in at the ER.

The same sequence of events took place just 24 hours later. Suzanne was on the phone with my pulmonologist as the EMTs wheeled me out of the house. I needed a different protocol than what was standard for the EMTs, and my doctor had to talk them through it. Throughout the night my pulmonologist from the Les Turner Foundation / Lois Insolia ALS Clinic was on the telephone with Suzanne, the EMTs and the emergency room doctors, guiding them to give me the best care they could. On her advice, I finally consented to the 40-mile drive to Northwestern Hospital so she could treat me directly.

Suzanne drove at something higher than the posted speed limits, fueled by adrenalin that overcame her fatigue of not having slept in more than 24 hours. I was half-coughing and choking the entire trip, nearly losing consciousness on several occasions. Suzanne, not being too familiar with the roads in downtown Chicago, parked where we normally would for a clinic visit. Once out of the van, I made a beeline at my wheelchair's full speed toward the emergency room, Suzanne running behind me. The ER staff had been advised of our impending arrival, and so we were taken to an exam room immediately where my vital signs formed a bleak picture. I was breathing at only 9% of normal capacity and carbon dioxide was building to toxic levels in my bloodstream.

Suzanne's eyes met mine in a look of profound love and deep concern; I wondered what it was going to feel like to tell her to let me go. I was so sorry for putting her through this emotional agony, so grateful for decades of loving partnership, so concerned for her future and the future of our children. My heart was aflame with love as I burned the image of her face into my spirit deep enough to last for eternity. She was thinking that we needed to get ready to say good-bye.

Suzanne tells me a nurse pounded my chest so hard to break up the congestion that my mom could hear it over the telephone. I remember none of that or of being transferred to the Intensive Care Unit with full-blown pneumonia. My pulmonologist started an aggressive course of treatment including massive antibiotics and all the respiratory therapies I should have been doing at home all along. Over the next several days, Suzanne considered sleeping on a gurney left in the hallway (the sleep chair in my room was very uncomfortable, but she wouldn't leave my side), my extended family gathered in the wing lounge to exchange Christmas gifts, we saw many friends who came to visit, Matthew took the imposing challenge of driving through downtown Chicago for the first time, solo, and we celebrated my birthday. In other words, people shared love, relationships were affirmed, and life blossomed. Thanks to the excellent care from the Northwestern staff and the diaphragm pacing system that had kept my diaphragm strong while so many of the other muscles involved with breathing had atrophied, my health was quickly restored, and the hospital stay came to a quick end.

We were again given the gift of time and, with it, the opportunity to reassess some of the decisions we had made. First, I now have — and use — all the equipment to support the respiratory therapy regimen. A flu shot is an annual not-to-be-missed appointment. I limit my social forays, sometimes wearing a mask, during cold and flu season. I am keenly aware of the fact that I am not invincible.

We were also given the opportunity to discuss extraordinary treatment measures in a much more nuanced light, especially the decision of whether or not to have a tracheostomy and get put on a mechanical ventilator. Before the bout with pneumonia, our decision had been to not take the vent because I believed that was a quality of life I couldn't accept. Now there are more dimensions to that question of quality of life — In what ways am I able to contribute to my family and communities? Are there major milestones coming up in the near future? What functional capacities do I still have, like can my legs still support my own weight?

In an odd sort of way, pneumonia turned out to be the Christmas gift I needed to make better decisions.

Walking Together

(This is a rally speech I gave before 5000 people at the Les Turner ALS Foundation's Eighth Annual Walk4Life)

There are those who would say "these are busy times; we can't expect people to participate in an event like this", and yet you are here, proving there is always time to love someone else.

And for today, there is hope.

And some would doubt our generosity in these troubled economic times, yet the outpouring of generosity here has exceeded all our expectations.

And for today, there is hope.

Some would say there is nothing we can do for ALS, yet today we provide funding to world-class researchers, clinicians, nurses, social workers, care coordinators and support people, providing today's care and unlocking tomorrow's secrets.

And for today, there is hope.

There is an empty sidewalk ahead of us today, reminding us that some would say ALS is a cold and lonely journey. But I look around at a sea of relatives and friends, old and new, with joy in their faces, anxious to overwhelm that lonely journey with love, care, and happiness.

And for today, there is hope.

And so I give thanks to all of you, for your love, support, and generosity. But mainly for your courage in accompanying me and my family in this journey, helping us to REclaim and PROclaim this precious gift —

that for today, there is hope.

Why Me?

There is a natural tendency to ask "Why me?" when the storms of life overwhelm us. Seeing some reason, some purpose in our situation helps put some order to the chaos. I have to confess that I have never asked this question in relation to getting ALS. Maybe that is partly because I don't particularly value order in my life, but it's probably more because I simply believe that God's once-perfect creation is now broken. Tragedy and illness happen in this broken world. Actually, why not me?

I have received many wonderful gifts in the midst of this storm. I am blessed with a healthier, happier approach to each day and family who cares enough to go through all the dirty and embarrassing tasks embedded in my everyday life. Various communities have rallied around me and my family, helping with household chores, meeting our spiritual needs, and raising money for our personal medical needs and for the Les Turner ALS Foundation. Most importantly, I experience God's presence in my life more fully.

I have another confession. I find the well-meaninged sentiments of people who say this is all part of God's plan irritating. God did not plan for people to get dreadful diseases or have terrible accidents or be victims of violence. Our world was created good, and there is nothing good about suffering. What I have found is that God has been present with me throughout, suffering and celebrating, pushing and holding, and always finding ways to invite me into a better life.

The situation where I do ask "Why me?" is when, week after week, I lose friends and Internet PALS to this awful illness. Most of them began having symptoms after me. Why am I still going, 11 years now, when others die in three to four years or even as quickly as 16 months? Should I feel guilty for surviving this long? Should I feel happy? Should I feel guilty for feeling happy? Do I feel happy for the inexplicable extra time I have with my family or guilty for all the extra years of work they have to endure to keep me going? Why do I deserve all this wonderful support when so many others are lonely and in need? In the end, what I feel is all of the above.

Life is not fair. And, as I have told my children on numerous occasions, for that I am deeply grateful. I shudder at what my life would have been like if I ever got what I truly deserved. I certainly would never have received God's forgiveness. In the end, I am grateful for God's grace and presence with me throughout my life, especially now. I can wait for answers to those other questions.

DREAMS

I dream to see the day when race, gender, age, faith, disability and sexual orientation play no part in national discourse- not because these issues are ignored but because they no longer have relevance in any political or social context.

I dream that we will measure our freedoms by the length and number of the chains on those most oppressed in our society.

I dream that we will measure personal success not by what we have accumulated but by what we have given away, and that we recognize whatever we have has come not only through our own efforts but also through those of others in our community, nation and world.

I dream that the horn of plenty will sound so that everyone might hear it.

I dream that our nation will measure its wealth by the lives lived by those least fortunate.

I dream that we see in others not the depth of their failure to live up to our expectations but the height of potential God sees for their lives.

Calling Out

"People do not fear death, only an inconsequential life." -

Bertolt Brecht

So now is the time of reckoning. It is time for you to take stock of the shells you have in your life and how you are using them. Are you hiding your gifts, polishing your life to make it look pretty and protecting your possessions and vulnerabilities? If so, you might also be one of the many who fear they may never find purpose and meaning in life.

Oysters, scallops and conches. Don't try denying them, for I know you have all three. Our world is filled with need, injustice, and division. I call on you to speak for the voiceless, to toil for those who cannot, to walk for those who have lost their strength. I call on you to hug the friendless, to create beauty in the wasteland, to comfort the struggling.

I call on you to give, serve, and bring people together. You will be a person of consequence, and you will have nothing to fear.

Made in the USA
Monee, IL
20 January 2022